DECEITFUL PEACE

Gerhart Niemeyer

DECEITFUL PEACE

A New Look at the Soviet Threat

ARLINGTON HOUSE

New Rochelle   New York

Library of Congress Catalog Card Number 69-16952

ISBN 0-87000-106-x

MANUFACTURED IN THE UNITED STATES OF AMERICA

THIS BOOK IS DEDICATED

TO

THE HONORABLE J. WILLIAM FULBRIGHT

U.S. Senator from Arkansas

Minus saepe erris si scias quid nescias

Preface

The badge they wear in America these days is named euphoria. It refers to what used to be the single overshadowing problem of United States policy: the Communist threat. The Cold War, so the official legend reads, is a thing of the past. "Cold warriors" are simply people who have not kept up with the times. They should have learned that we have moved from "old myths" to "New realities," that theirs are the "outworn reflexes and concepts" of happily bygone days. There is a hint in all of this that the Cold War even in the past stemmed merely from our minds, that there never was an enemy of the United States and that neither our security nor that of our allies was ever seriously in danger. The official euphoria, however, which dismisses the past of defense-mindedness with amused contempt, needs not to dwell on such problems. Suffice it to assert that the Soviet Union is fast moving toward liberalism, that our social system and theirs are converging to a point of close mutual resemblance, that the Kremlin has embraced peace as its main objective even at the risk of losing its closest and most powerful ally, that we are now cooperating with Moscow in many areas, and will have much more of the same.

Those who do not share this optimism happen to be out of favor and regarded as not fit to print. Their views are not based on different facts, for the salient information about Communism is fully accessible to all. The facts, however, do not for them add up to the same conclusions, for they see them in the light of different assumptions. These assumptions turn, above all, on the nature of Communism as an ideological movement, and on the probability of its evolution toward some kind of liberal-democratic mode of government. Such evolution, they feel, is not probable, and, what is more, not indicated by the known facts. Thus they are deeply concerned about what they consider an official illusion of peace and point to massive erosions in our ramparts that have resulted therefrom. "There is a crisis because there is no crisis" said Raymond Aron, coining a brilliant formula for a situation in which the apparent absence of an overt threat can inflict deep wounds and cause serious weaknesses.

This book attempts to put before the reader the assumptions about Communism that preclude any relaxation of our political or military stance. The view that the threat continues, more serious now that we have been sucked into cooperating with it, is based on the same set of facts that is known to the other side. In other words, here is a situation in which a real discussion may emerge, because our country will go this way or that, to a glorious destiny or to ignominious failure, according to its capacity of comprehending realities and grasping principles. The view here presented does not usually find easy access to newspaper and magazine columns and is frequently buried under waves of scorn. In putting down what is, mildly speaking, an unpopular version of things, the writer had in mind the case of a man who, many thousand years ago, also came forward to warn of a mortal threat when his compatriots were already celebrating peace. He and his sons were crushed by the snakes, and they went to their doom. Let us hear the story in Vergil's own words:

In sight of Troy there's an island, a well-known
                                        island, Tenedos—
Thither the Greeks sailed out, and hid on its desolate coast.
This was evacuation, we thought—they had sailed for
    Greece.
So all Troy threw off the chains of her long anguish.
We opened the gates, we enjoyed visiting the Greek
    camp,
Viewing the derelict positions on the abandoned beaches . . .
Some of us gaped at the gift—so deadly—the Greeks had
                                        left for
Minerva, and its stupendous bulk. Thymoetes first,
Either from treachery or because Troy's fate now was sealed,
Urged that the horse he brought through the walls and
                                        placed in our citadel.
But Capys and all those of sounder views recommended
Hurling it into the sea or setting fire to it, as some
Booby-trap of the Greeks and not to be trusted . . .
Then out in front of them all, hundreds straggling behind
    him,
In a great temper Laocoön came tearing down from the citadel,
Crying from far:
                Citizens, are you all stark mad?
Do you really believe our foes are gone? Do you imagine
Any Greek gift is guileless? Is that your idea of Ulysses?

This thing of wood conceals Greek soldiers, or else it is
A mechanism designed against our walls—to pry into
Our homes and to bear down on the city; sure, some trick
Is there. No, you must never feel safe with the horse,
                                              Trojans.
Whatever it is, I distrust the Greeks, even when they
                              are generous . . .

Just then another event, the most alarming yet,
Befell us wretches, muddling still further our hooded minds.
Laocoön, whom we'd elected by lot as Neptune's priest,
Was sacrificing a great bull at the official altar,
When over the tranquil deep, from Tenedos, we saw—
Telling it makes me shudder—twin snakes with immense
        coils . . .

Went straight for Laocoön. First, each snake knotted itself
Round the body of one of Laocoön's small sons, hugging him
                                              tight
In its coils, and cropped the piteous flesh with its fangs.
                              Next thing,
They fastened upon Laocoön . . .
Embrace him, their heads and throats powerfully poised
                        above him . . .

Then, my god! a strange panic crept into our people's
                              fluttering
Hearts: they argued Laocoön had got what he deserved . . .
"Bring the horse to Minerva's shrine! Pray for her good will!"
All of our people shouted.
We cut into our walls, laid open the heart of the city . . .

                  Not a sound from the Trojans, supine
Along the walls, tired out, in the embrace of sleep.
And now the main Greek army was moving from Tenedos
In fleet formation. . . .

The horse disgorged, the men
Burst revelling forth from its hollow flank into the
fresh air—. . .
They broke out over a city in drunken sleep. . . .
Troy's tower is falling, falling.
The Aeneid, Book II (trans. C. Day Lewis)

Contents

14

DECEITFUL PEACE

CHAPTER 1

———————————··•⌣∾⌢•··———————————

The Meaning
of Communist Ideology

Communist Ideology: Fact or Fiction?

In an oblique way, the question of Communist ideology is pivotal to American policy and the destiny of our civilization. Nobody denies the fact that the relation between the U.S.A. and the USSR dominates world affairs: the question concerns rather the nature of this relation, and that in turn the further question of the nature of the Moscow regime. We think we know ourselves and our intentions; we take ourselves for granted; it is the other side that is the variable in the equation. Also, no one denies that the Moscow regime consists of Communists, so everything turns on one's estimate of what kind of people Communists are. Since 1963, the American government has officially embraced an estimate that identifies Communists either with "the Russian people, who abhor war," or with us in the sense that their interests are parallel or identical to ours, or with an inevitable trend toward liberalism that again sees the Communists and us on the same bandwagon of history, or with Russia's national interest in stability and security. The alternative view identifies Communists as people with a purpose of world revolution, or with Russian expansionism, or with a propensity to war and violent conflict, or with a design for empire. The military capability of the rulers of Russia is not a major issue, although even that every once in a while becomes a bone of contention. "The nature of the Moscow regime" thus means the motivation of the Kremlin rulers, their way of looking at the rest of the world, in short, their animus.

The Communist ideology is the central problem in this debate, for, again, nobody denies the existence of an idea system that is characteristic of the Communist Party of the Soviet Union and Communists in general. The question is only whether that idea system has anything to do with the motives or actions of Communists in the Kremlin, or whether it once was, but is no longer, the epitome of Communist intent, or whether there still is such a thing as a recognizable Communist ideology. In this complex of questions, the terms "ideology" and "ideological" are used with a number of different meanings. Some understand an ideology to mean any kind of belief or set of principles, as opposed to a purely pragmatic approach to things; other meanings of "ideology" include an idea system that one carries along, as it were, like a Sunday suit, not really for business, or a set of propositions to which one turns every time before making a decision. When we ask ourselves whether Communists are ideologically motivated, we mean sometimes "strict to the letter of their classical authors," or "unrealistic because of preconceived ideas," or "irrational in their attitudes" or "dogmatic and unbending." Frequently, a discussion of this question is unfruitful because the participants miss one another's meaning and bypass each other's arguments.

The two poles in these meanings of the word "ideology" are an idea system and a type of attitude or outlook. There is an idea system pertaining to the Communist Party; it is contained in the writings of Lenin, Marx, and Engels and summarized in a number of Stalin's works, and it is thus clearly identifiable and knowable. The question then is whether this idea system engenders any specifically Communist attitudes. Are people who have accepted this idea system different from others, do they have a peculiar outlook, an orientation that engenders a collective will separating them from others? The answers to such questions are difficult to establish. They involve more than behavior and thus "more than meets the eye." In a sense, they hinge on a general probability. Those who deny the effectiveness of the Communist ideology or even its existence do so on grounds of general improbability: one cannot assume that anyone seriously believes in an idea system that seems to him irrational in its assumptions or conclusions, therefore one must assume that the ideology in Communist Party circles is mere window dressing. There is only one way of establishing the general possibility of an ideological orientation: one must oneself delve into ideology and follow its contortions, probing whether one could oneself become a captive of its logic, given favorable circumstances. In other words, if there is such a thing as an ideological sickness of the mind, one must allow oneself to be affected by it for the purpose of finding out what is its efficacy.

Alienation and Revolution

The Communist ideology is very complex and its statement has taken many volumes of writing by Marx, Engels, and Lenin. We shall take it up at this point in a severely abbreviated form by grouping its leading concepts around certain core purposes, namely, Marx's idea of evil and redemption from evil, his view of history as a knowable sequence of various "phases" or "stages," and his evaluation of the "present-day society."

Throughout the entire period of recorded history, Marx claimed, man has not lived a human life but rather vegetated in a distorted mode of existence. Marx's name for this perversion of life was "alienation." Marx saw man as having his essence in labor, which is his relation with nature. Just as Aristotle said, "more than anything else, reason *is* man," so Marx might have said, "more than anything else, labor *is* man." Thus, if the labor process and labor's product were not controlled by man, he could not be himself. According to Marx, this was the case in a situation where man produced in response to demands made on him by others, or by the market. Where labor was subjected to "alien powers" like the market, man could not be himself, said Marx. In an "alienated" society, man is a fragment, dependent on alien powers that govern his life, and this condition is reflected in ideas which are separate from reality and thus false. For Marx, religion was a product of an "alienated" existence, philosophy is "alienated" thinking, and the state is "alienated" authority. Thus in the present-day society everything is false, despotic, and anti-human. As opposed to this condition, Marx envisaged a future society in which man, albeit only collectively, would have full control of his labor process and products, and in which "theory" would be united with "action."

The great importance of this whole view is the stark separation of the here from the there, and the remedy or connection between the two which Marx conceived. That connection is revolution, the opposite of evolution. Not every revolution would do, but only a "radical revolution" that would destroy every vestige of the existing system and not even "leave the pillars of the house standing." Such total destruction requires force, and the requisite force can be found only in the masses. Here is how Marx defined what he needed: "a class with *radical chains*, . . . a sphere which has universal character by its universal suffering and claims no *particular right* because no *particular wrong* but *wrong generally* is perpetrated against it . . . which, in a word, is the *complete loss* of man, and hence can win itself only through the *complete re-winning of man*" (*Economic and Philosophical Manuscripts of 1844*). Let us watch closely what is going on here. Marx envisions a radical change of everything that exists, from which man, hitherto not himself, would emerge complete, finally human, whole, and free. He believes that force is needed for this change, and that force resides in the masses. He is looking for insurrectionist masses, but they must have the special quality that their insurrection will benefit not just themselves alone but all of mankind. Therefore Marx postulates a social element in which all humanity is annihilated and infers that, when this element rises up to overthrow its oppressors, its deed will liberate, redeem, and complete man in his full humanity. Having thus defined the nature of "radical revolution" and conceived of an historical mission for the masses behind that event, he casts around for some element in reality to which he can assign this mission. His eyes come to rest on "the proletariat," a class that had received its name only shortly before and that was then enjoying the *mystique de la gauche,* the feeling that who or whatever is most on the Left is by definition the essence of "the people." It is therefore not a feeling of compassion, or an experience of suffering, that drove Marx to espouse the cause of the common man. He never did espouse that cause and was scornful of all who saw the proletariat above all as the "suffering class." For Marx, the proletariat is above all a force, the force "that holds the future in its hands," that has the power requisite for total negation and total destruction of everything that is, and thereby can save mankind. Marx looked upon the proletariat as the element of negative power that is the political reality of negative thought. In that sense, the proletariat differs from all other revolutionary forces in history. Marx calls it the "only really revolutionary class." He means that the proletariat alone does not seek any advantage for itself, that as its mission is to destroy totally in order to liberate completely, it will never stop at any partial gain but rather go on negating, combating, subverting every bit of social order until the human condition is totally transfigured. "Permanent revolution" is what Marx demands of the proletariat. Its mission is irreconcilable and unmitigated struggle. The result of that struggle—Marx promised to the world—will be an eventual society free from class rule, exploitation, poverty, war, yes from all evil and the causes of evil. Then, at last, man will be fully man, no longer a fragment of himself. His thought and his action will be united. He will control the forces of society that hitherto enslaved him. Individuality and collectivity will merge in flawless harmony.

The first major argument in Communist ideology, then, is that the present as well as the past is inhuman and totally worthless, and that a specific class, the proletariat, has the power to redeem mankind from all the evils it has endured in history. The second part of the structure consists in what the Marxists call the "laws of history." According to Marx, the class struggle is the mechanism of change. There is always a ruling class, he said. It has power in society inasmuch as it owns the means of production, so that political rule is really nothing but a façade for the realities of property. But economic developments bring about the strengthening of a new and upcoming class which begins to produce in new ways, by means of a novel kind of property. Eventually that class will become strong enough to overthrow the hitherto ruling class, which means that it will replace the former "superstructure" of government, laws, and ideas with a new one, one corresponding to its novel type of property and production. By this process mankind inevitably moves from one type of society to another, according to Marx. The underlying forces of change are economic and involuntary, but the class struggle itself is political and conscious, with revolution climaxing it as a political explosion of the entire structure. On this showing, the Communist ideology now distinguishes five main types of society through which human history is bound to move: primitive society, slaveholding society, feudal society, bourgeois society, and socialist society. The concept "laws of history" means that these "phases" must follow each other in this order, that the succession from one to the other is the necessary path of history, so that

no matter in what phase men find themselves, they can and
must know that their ultimate destination is the socialist
climax. As the "laws of history" became the most important element in the Marxist structure, concepts of impersonal forces replaced concepts of humanity. Most
important, the desired revolution of the proletariat can
now be seen as an event that history's laws will bring
about. In the present, the ruling class is destined eventually to be overthrown by its "slaves," the proletariat. Thus
the end of bourgeois society is decreed by the "laws of
history," and the future is inevitably that society which
will grow out of the proletariat's victory: socialism, or
Communism.*

Present, Future, and Struggle in Between

In a sense, these two main parts already encompass the

* The distinction between socialism and Communism frequently puzzles people.
Rightly so, because this is a pair of concepts that is used with many different meanings.
One can distinguish the following:
   a) In a basic sense, Communists speak of the future society as socialist, as distinct
from capitalist. But they differentiate between various phases of development *after* the
proletariat has overthrown the bourgeoisie and abolished private ownership of the
means of production. The first and lower phase of the new society, which is still beset
with the "eggshells" of its origin, they call "socialism"; the higher phase, in which all
their expectations would finally be realized, is "Communism."
   b) In the middle of the 19th century, when Marx formulated his ideas, quite a few
other socialist movements existed in France, England, and other places. Marx then
called his own version of socialism "Communist," and distinguished it from other
brands by characterizing it as "scientific" and the others "utopian."
   c) Between 1903 and 1919, a split developed within the broad Marxist movement
between those who with Lenin wanted a small, tightly disciplined Communist Party that
would commit itself to an irreconcilable class struggle and an eventual dictatorial
regime, and others who wanted socialism to come as a result of mass pressure and the
majority weight of people converted to the socialist idea. The former, after the Russian
revolution and the foundation of the Comintern, called themselves "Communists"
and split off from the others who in many countries called themselves "social democrats" or merely "socialists."
   d) "Socialism" is a term also invoked by movements arising after Marx which did
not follow Marx's lead but aimed at an eventual socialist society through legislative and
administrative steps. Particularly the Fabian Society in England thus professed "socialism" in a sense quite distinct from Marxism and much more oriented toward certain
government policies than a revolution of the proletariat. In America, many of the
elements behind the New Deal, Great Society, etc., are socialist in this sense.

Marxist message. But Marx's *Capital*, written after these ideas had already been formulated, added what might be considered a third part: a sociological analysis of the "bourgeois" society as a basis for its total condemnation. The explanation begins with the concept "commodity production," i.e., the production of goods mainly for the purpose of trade. This is the pattern of production characterizing "bourgeois society," the "present-day society." The laws of commodity production, particularly the laws of value, also apply to labor, which in the bourgeois society is a commodity like others, offered on the market and bought at its value. The value of labor, like that of all other commodities, is determined by the labor time required to produce it. As applied to labor itself, that means its value as a commodity is the equivalent of the labor time required to feed, house, and clothe a laborer and his family. Thus the price of labor, i.e., wages, will tend to hug closely the subsistence level, Marx maintained. The next step is Marx's most important explanation of exploitation through the concept of "surplus value." The worker, says Marx, sells his labor power to the capitalist at its market value, i.e., the cost of subsistence, in the free market. The contract is for a day's work. Now it takes a worker only a fraction of a day to produce the amount of value that corresponds to his own subsistence. That means that during the rest of the day he will produce value over and above what it has cost the employer to hire him. This value over and above is what Marx called "surplus value." Surplus value, according to Marx, is the sole source of capital, for it alone creates profit for the employer. Thus Marx indicts, not the individual capitalist, but the entire system for a) perpetuating itself by means of value created by the worker for which the worker has not been paid, b) keeping the worker at subsistence level and thus building the structure of wealth on the poverty of the "wage-slaves," c) condemning the workers, who alone produce surplus value, to create the chains by which they are fettered, despite the most complete legal and political freedom. According to Marx, the entire bourgeois society rests on the sole foundation of exploitation and thus stands condemned beyond any hope of redemption. Marx also used his economic-sociological analysis allegedly to prove that the capitalist system of production is so rent by inner contradictions that it must eventually rush to its own collapse, through a series of ever worsening economic crises, through the steadily worsening misery of ever increasing masses, through the gradual but inexorable diminution of the profit rate. His indictment of exploitation is powerful but faulty on a number of counts, the main one being his contrived narrowing-down of the argument. Exploitation is possible among human beings every time someone on account of his needs or weaknesses is dependent on someone else. In many such situations persons take advantage of the other's dependence and build up their own position. The most widespread practice of exploitation occurs in sexual relations, but it is widespread also within families, among friends, and in other relations. Most important, though, side by side with exploitation there are features in human relations that recognize man as an end in himself, lift him above and protect him against exploitation. It is significant that Marx, in the midst of his total condemnation of bourgeois society, acknowledged the ten-hour bill, passed in England in 1847, as labor's "Magna Charta," but did so in a passing note and never stopped to consider the implication of this statement for the validity of his indictment.

Tedious though this necessarily brief survey may be, it must suffice to explain the simplifications that can be said to govern the Communist mind. They are a characteristic mixture of ideas claiming to set forth a hitherto concealed knowledge of society, the motion of history, and principles of action. The entire structure rests on three foundations: the judgment pronounced on bourgeois society, the promise of eventual salvation, and the guarantee of certain and reliable knowledge of all of this.

1. The bourgeois society is considered the epitome of injustice and evil. Its system is essentially nothing but exploitation. Even though it may pay the workers relatively well, it still exploits them. Its liberties and immunities are merely window dressing and sham. Its morality, art, literature amount to nothing more than hypocrisy. Its law and politics constitute self-interest embodied in institutions of power. Capitalism, in the eyes of Communists, is to blame for whatever we find wrong in the world. Communist ideology, however, narrows its general condemnation of evil down to a concrete target: the bourgeoisie, or to one even more specific: the monopolists of Wall Street, whose overthrow would mark the end of all wrongs in history. Thus man's hope and love for the good can translate themselves into practice only if they turn into a struggle against capitalist power, or as Lenin later identified it, imperialism. On Marx's unquestioned authority, Communists claim that no decent man can deny himself to that cause. He who remains even lukewarm must be a coward or a weakling; he who stays on the sidelines can be no better than a fool or a knave.

2. By contrast with the total evil of the present, Communist ideology promises a future of total good that is supposed to emerge after the complete defeat of the class enemy. By definition, socialism is pictured as an age without oppression, exploitation, poverty, and war. It is a society of unselfish men and hence without conflicts. This is the ultimate goal, the vision that justifies all Communist action. For the Communists consider themselves the force that does battle so that the vision can become reality. The socialist age cannot be made at will, it is subject to the "laws of history," but by virtue of those laws it will be the result of the struggle the proletariat wages against its bourgeois masters. The proletariat is "the class that holds the future in its hands." Thus all forward-looking men, all progressive elements have an ensign to which they can repair: the banner of the proletariat, history's appointed instrument. Any decent man, in Communist eyes, has the duty to fight the bourgeois society, but no man can be called intelligent unless he does so by supporting "the proletariat" and its party, the Communist Party.

3. As far as Communists are concerned, this message need not to be taken on faith. For them, the inhumanity and rottenness of the bourgeois society have been objectively proved by Marx's analysis, and the good of the future is no mere hope but a "scientific" certainty, rooted in the knowledge of the "laws of history." Historical materialism is considered the key to this knowledge. Communists, who have inherited Marx's historical materialism, are the only ones in a position to know mankind's destiny with positive assurance. It is by historical necessity that the bourgeois society will spread its system over the entire globe, the system of imperialism. By the same neces-

sity, this system will engender "its own gravediggers," the revolutionary masses, who will, when the time comes, overthrow the bourgeois rule and thus pave the way for the new socialist society. "Communists must know that in any event the future is theirs," said Lenin, and Khrushchev later added: "We shall bury you; the red flag will fly over the entire world." This is the expression of a certainty derived from the conviction that Marxism is a science, the "science" of history, and that its conclusions are no mere wishes but facts which, although still in the future, appear as good as consummated.

Changing Details and Unchanging Essence

A total condemnation of the present society, a concrete target for one's righteous anger, a promise of future perfection in this world, and organized struggle as the road to that future: here are the permanent ingredients of the Communist outlook. This combination of moral judgment, noble vision, and an allegedly scientific proof provides a complete meaning of life, a direction for one's activities, and the possibility of engaging in a virtuous cause. One must remember all these elements, in order to understand Communism. Many misconceptions stem from focusing on only one or two of these elements and forgetting about the others. One of the most widespread misconceptions sees Communism as essentially, nay, exclusively, a system of historical materialism. On this showing one is then inclined to demand of Communists that they live up to the strictures of a materialist construction of history, and, if they fail to do so, to declare that they are no longer ideologically motivated. One then tends to overlook the fact that historical materialism plays no more than an auxiliary role in the Communist mind, that its main function is to provide the certainty of the promised future, and that no Communist has ever slavishly or even reverently adhered to its biddings. Historical materialism is important mainly in that it dispenses the Communists from the requirement, and the risk, of faith. They take historical materialism as the guarantee that their belief is a "science," that the moral indictment of capitalism is objectively true, that there are "laws of history," and that the proletarian revolution is not a postulate but a fact. Historical materialism helps them know against whom to struggle, whom or what to join in the struggle, and to be positively certain of the eventual outcome.

In other words, the Communist ideology, a most complex structure, has parts that are of minor importance and parts that are essential, and the less important parts can be slighted, changed, and even partly discarded. This becomes evident to anyone who follows the development of the ideology. Lenin himself introduced changes that strike one as downright un-Marxist, *if one assumes that Marxism is historical materialism.* Lenin envisaged and planned a proletarian-led revolution in a country which, according to his own statements, was just moving into the "bourgeois" phase of history, in which, therefore, there could only be a nascent proletariat and a budding capitalism. He invented the principle of a Communist seizure of power with the peasantry as the main numerical support. He played down the "consciousness" of the proletariat that would arise from its living conditions, and played up the "theory" that came from knowing Marxism. He began to apply the term "bourgeoisie" to the peasantry, something that never would have occurred to Marx. In other words, he violated many of the supposed dictates of historical materialism as applied to Russia. In so doing Lenin created what is now known as the Communist ideology, around which he planned and organized the Communist Party. This movement was and is an activist, militant enterprise founded squarely on what has been the very core of Marxism. Whatever the rationalizing details, the central ideas of Marxism are that capitalism is the epitome of evil and must be destroyed, that the class struggle against the bourgeoisie will end in the victory "of the proletariat" from which will evolve a future socialist society, and that these things are bound to happen by virtue of the "laws of history" which have been scientifically established by Marxism. This central motive was the single force in Lenin's actions, while the other details of the Marxist system could be altered to suit the circumstances, or even used to defeat one's fellow Marxist opponents. One has only to look for the emphases in Lenin to perceive what it was that governed his will. When Bernstein, in sober reasoning, restated the Marxist message as class struggle for higher justice but without eventual revolution, Lenin insisted on the irreconcilability of the class struggle and the total destruction of the bourgeois society. As far as the moral indictment of capitalism is concerned, Lenin thought of a number of epithets that had not occurred to Marx: he called capitalists "parasites," "coupon-clippers," "wire-pullers," "imperialists," adding two more to the list of capitalism's evils that Marx had set up, namely, colonialism and international war. It was Lenin who dug up, more or less from oblivion, those writings of Marx which center on the problems of protracted class struggle and its power

strategy, to wit, the *Address to the Communist League*
(1850), the *Class Struggles in France* (1850), the *18th
Brumaire* (1852), the *Civil War in France* (1871), and the
Critique of the Gotha Programme (1875). What is more,
Lenin's own theorizing efforts focused not on applications
of historical materialism, but on the requirements of militant struggle against the class enemy. Thus he created the
principle of the Communist "vanguard" Party and its relation to the masses, the scheme of alliances with non-
proletarian masses (the peasantry, and later on, the
nationalist bourgeoisie in semi-colonial countries), and the
concept of international politics as class struggle with the
goal of overthrowing capitalism. He developed the idea of
the dictatorship of the proletariat which Marx had only
briefly mentioned, and he elaborated principles of operation that would guide Communists in the maze of political
relations with their class enemies. In all of this, the will to
struggle to the victorious end, the ultimate hope that constitutes the meaning of this struggle, and the clear focus on
a single enemy as the target are the invariables, and whatever calculations enter from historical materialism are the
variables.

The Communist ideology, in other words, is quite compatible with changes in many details, including details that
some Marxists and nearly all non-Marxists regard as essential. For instance, the concept of a class enemy is part
of the core, but the social definition of that class enemy can
change even to the point where the original "bourgeois"
quality is no longer recognizable. Similarly, the idea of a
revolution attributed to the proletariat is essential, but it
is possible to shift the designation of certain social elements as belonging to this revolution from the proletariat

to others, for instance, from "proletariat" to "toilers" or "the masses," or "all oppressed people," or "the peasants," or "the Negroes," as long as the dogma of irreconcilable class struggle is still preserved. The perfect society of the future is an unchanging motivation, but it is possible to postpone the realization of this future, or to modify its particular features, in so far as they are anticipated, as long as one still visualizes that future in diametrical opposition to the evil present. Even historical materialism as such can be read in a number of different ways. It would not occur to any Communist to conceive of it as strict determinism that admits of no role for the political will. But it can be understood to mean that a radical social transformation can come only when the conditions are ripe, or, alternatively, that the Communist must take into account all existing social forces and their full strength in the social fabric, so that for the duration of this strength Communists must conceal their purposes, accept allies, operate partly underground, and be ready to compromise. Materialism has suggested to some Marxists (notably Lenin's opponents, the Mensheviks) an obligation to refrain from revolutionary action until the "fullness of time." Lenin himself saw in materialism chiefly a counsel of caution against revolutionary utopianism, a reminder that the business of a revolution cannot be Simon-pure in its principles. It would be a serious mistake to look at this variety of conceptions and conclude that Communists or others have used Marx's theory in a spirit of sheer expediency. On the contrary, it is possible to say that even Marx himself did not take his own historical materialism very seriously, at least not as seriously as his will to revolutionary struggle, and that even for him historical materialism was mainly a

source of certainty, conviction, and the general color of
the main ideological argument. There are no instances
where Marxist leadership resorted to historical materialism as if it were a textbook for practice. Everywhere it
functions like a general but changeable attribute of the
revolutionary will, something of which one is aware, but
in a free manner.

One should understand Marxist-Leninist ideology as
centering in a core of goals and basic assumptions that is
surrounded by layers of rationalizations in which there is
considerable room for creative changes, adaptation to circumstances, and manipulations. Hence Marxists, without
abandoning the common core, can become involved in
sharp differences of opinion. On the other hand, the
ideology also makes it possible for someone with sufficient
power to clamp on this or that interpretation the fatal
"anti-revolutionary" label and thereby to destroy his opponents. Beyond that, the flexibility of the ideology enables Communists to use the ideological concepts in a
two-faced way, manipulating them for political infighting
while at the same time heeding them for guidance and
internal unity. This complexity is hard to grasp, and it may
help us to recall the example of Louis XI of France, a most
devout and most suspicious monarch, who on his deathbed
had the Pope send him a saintly hermit to pray for his
recovery, but at the same time had spies test the holy man
to see that he was not a charlatan. In this sense one should
not rashly conclude that the bending of the ideology to
power ends within the Party reveals an underlying cynicism, any more than Louis's suspicion of a saint's prayers
canceled out his faith in salvation through Christ. Nor
should one mistake this kind of use of the ideology for a

subjection of the mind to political emotions. Communists are trained to make their emotions serve their consciously held ideas of the world and the Communist purpose in it. The Communist knows that what makes him and the Party is the ideology; but that precisely also suggests to him the possibility of using the ideology as his tool, accessory, or smokescreen. These contradictions are rooted not in the ideology as such but in human nature.

CHAPTER 2

Communist Attitudes

There is some truth in the disdain many people have for the question of Communist ideology: If it were no more than a web of strange and semirational ideas spun in the heads of *déraciné* intellectuals, the Communist ideology would not concern us very much. In politics what matters is action, and the attitudes from which actions flow. If it did not induce typical attitudes, the Communist ideology could be treated as a purely academic subject. Communism, however, is an activist movement; an ideology has translated itself into patterns of obedience, commitment, fears, hopes, hatreds, and habits. One can speak of Communists, as distinct from other people, not only in terms of membership in an organization, or of adherence to certain general propositions, but also in terms of evaluations, relations, impulses that typically differ from those of non-Communists. In other words, there is such a thing as a Communist man, even to a higher degree than one can speak of an American man, a European man, a Mediterranean man, or a modern man. Communism is the organized power creating and employing typical attitudes. In so far as Communism must be called a source of political disturbance, both in Communist-controlled countries and in the world at large, this peculiar quality can be understood only through the attitudes characteristic of Communists. In this sense, the term "ideological" refers less to the system of ideas as such, than to the abnormal quality of the attitudes that have been cultivated by organized Communism.

Living in the Future

Probably the deepest difference between Communist and normal attitudes lies in the orientation in time. Normally people consider themselves living in the present, rooted in the past, and seeing ahead of them an open future with a variety of possibilities which puts the matter of realization up to their choice. Communists, by contrast, consider themselves at home primarily in the future, which for them is essentially closed rather than open. From that point of view, the present is mainly a path of transition to the future, and it is the future rather than the present to which alone they attribute value and significance. This attitude they term "progressive," while the attitude of people who live chiefly in the present is by Communists deemed "bourgeois" and "reactionary." They demand that the present be lived in as if it were the straight path to a foregone conclusion. It is strange but true that in Communist eyes the future appears more real than the present. A typical example of this attitude is reported by Hellmut Gollwitzer, a German theologian who after the war remained as a captive in Russia. In his book, *Und führen, wohin du nicht willst* (1954), he reports about the curious enthusiasm that can animate Communists in the face of present conditions that would make other people shudder. If one is astonished at this discrepancy, they reply: "You must see this dialectically," or "You have no idea what man can still become!" A professor in Russia lectured to them, the captives, as follows:

> If you say "this is an old, badly painted barrack wall" then you judge "metaphysically," i.e. you make absolute a moment of the present. But if you say "this is a perfectly white, beautiful new wall," then you may be wrong as far as the present moment is concerned, because the wall is not yet white and beautiful, but dialectically speaking you are right, because that is what it will be tomorrow. If after returning (to Germany) you tell people at home that the Soviet people live in old, vermin-infested barracks, you will have told a lie, even though this is still so to a large extent; but if you tell them that the Soviet people live in beautiful new homes, you will be telling the truth, although today only a few live this way. To recognize the to-morrow in the today—that is to "see dialectically." (Pp.113 ff.)

Another account of "dialectic thinking" comes from Professor Carlo Schmid, the German statesman who, in the company of Chancellor Adenauer, visited Moscow in 1955:

> At one time, Chancellor Adenauer said: "But, gentlemen, nobody knows what will be in a hundred years!" "Read Karl Marx, then you *will* know." This was not meant as a joke but entirely seriously. And another example showed us what dialectic is: While walking about, we talked about the population policy of the Soviet Union. Marshal Bulga-

nin told me: "The commodity we lack above all is man-power. Therefore we want children and more children and still more children. That is why we encourage early marriages and people to have babies. We have abolished all laws passed in former disordered times concerning birth control. We punish abortion severely." One hour later, we talked in a different context about China, and he said: "Yes, that is a difficult situation. Six hundred million people whom they can hardly feed, plus an annual population increase of twelve million who must also be fed. Fortunately, the Chinese have adopted good laws, laws about birth control. Abortion is legal, interruption of pregnancy is encouraged, and so on." I replied: "But, Mr. Prime Minister, isn't that most curious, now black and then white? A while ago, you denounced Malthusianism!" "Yes," he said, "don't you know what dialectic is?" (Speech of October 28, 1955)

In the textbook which until 1953 was continuously used for political indoctrination (the so-called *Short Course*), Stalin summed up dialectical materialism not only as a philosophical proposition, but also as an attitude:

The dialectical method regards as important primarily not that which at the given moment seems to be durable and yet is already beginning to die away, but that which is arising and developing, even though at the given moment it may not appear to be durable; for the dialectical method considers invincible only that which is arising and developing.

Toward the present, i.e., anything that now exists, the Communists maintain a profound suspicion on principle, for they consider it dominated by the influences of the bourgeoisie which, as Lenin put it, "encircle the proletariat on every side with a petty-bourgeois atmosphere which permeates and corrupts the proletariat." The Communists believe that they, by contrast, represent not what man is now but "what may become of man." The disdain of the Communists for the present, and their conviction that they are the army of the future are the most fundamental of all Communist attitudes. A German natural scientist and Sovietologist who regularly attends meetings at which both Western and Soviet scientists are present, told the author how he once approached a Russian colleague and asked him pointblank how he, an intelligent and educated man, could find it in him to put up with all the Communist regimentation, distortion of truth, indoctrination, and despotism. The Russian did not protest but, after a thoughtful pause, replied slowly: "Because I love mankind." He meant that every evil stemming from Communism in the present was justified by the future which he, too, regarded as an unquestionable certainty towards which Communists alone constitute the transition. It did not occur to him that this living in a dream-future rather than in the given present doomed him to a dream-land existence.

The Party: Spiritual Home and Font of Truth

Feeling himself a stranger in the present, the Communist clings all the more tightly to the one institution in the present that to him is justified by the future: the Communist Party. Communist attitudes regarding the Party differ decisively from those which normal people have toward political parties. Normally, parties are organizations through which people, within the larger whole of the entire society, pursue specific political purposes: policies differing from those of a rival party, personal advancement to positions of power, possibly even personal financial advantages. The ends are thus set by citizens, individually or in groups, and the parties are instruments considered suitable for the promotion of such ends. The very word "party" befits this attitude: it denotes a purpose and an organization considered a part of something larger, thereby acknowledging other similar parts, a set of differing purposes vying with each other for public acceptance. At the same time, the word implies that whatever in each citizen is party-minded is no more than a part of him. Being a Republican in this country is not tantamount to a full description of a man; he knows himself to be also an American, a Christian or Jew, man of the West, a human being.

In Communist eyes, on the other hand, the Party is not an instrument of some purpose that Communists espouse among other purposes, but rather the total mold of their present existence, and thus a whole, indeed the only conceivable whole, rather than a part. In an otherwise chaotic and inhuman present, the Party is the movement toward the future, in visible shape. A Communist does not embrace the Party on account of its policies. The opposite is true: the Party's policies change, not infrequently from black to white and again to black with dizzying speed, and the Communist will adapt himself to the shifting policies as to something that is *not* of the essence of the Party. He will make every effort to suppress his objections to this or that turn of the Party line, and to explain and justify it, only to contradict his own arguments the day after a new turn has been taken. "It must not be thought," observes Frank S. Meyer, himself a former Communist, "that the

Communist subjectively considers what he is doing as avoiding traps or manipulating words. He regards it much more seriously—as an intellectual discipline absolutely necessary to arrive at truth. The necessity of learning to thread one's way through such dangers, therefore, contributes greatly in training the Communist cadre not merely to follow 'the line of the Party' but to understand it and deeply accept it." (*The Moulding of Communists*, 1961, p.31) The Party, then, is not regarded as an instrument for a previously set purpose, or for an end conceived spontaneously by citizens. Rather the Party itself is the purpose to which the Communist as an entire human being attaches and molds himself. Meyer reports a number of cases in which the Party demanded, and the individual Communist accomplished, a radical change of his personal life so that he could be of use to the Party. It is obvious that in this kind of relationship no rival loyalty can possibly be tolerated, so that a Communist must look on himself as a Communist first and last, and cannot, besides being a Communist, also be a Christian, a Russian, or a human being. George Lukács, the prominent Hungarian Communist intellectual, once commented to one of the author's friends: "I would rather eat dirt than separate myself from the movement." And Trotsky, at the time when he was being pushed out of the Party, stated his attitude: "One can be right only with the Party and through the Party because history has not created any other way for the realization of one's rightness."

One can say that the Communist Party is a unique phenomenon by virtue of the attitude of Communists with regard to this institution. That attitude was defined and explained by Piatakov, a member of the Trotsky opposition who, having been expelled from the Party in 1927, publicly capitulated and retracted his previous views. Shortly afterwards, a former Menshevik had a conversation with Piatakov in which he accused him of lack of moral courage. At that point, Piatakov, in a state of great emotional excitement, replied with a long tirade.

> "The essential Lenin," he said, "was not to be found in the creator of NEP and in the leader's last articles. . . . The real Lenin was the man who had the courage to make a proletarian revolution first, and then to set about creating the objective conditions theoretically necessary as a preliminary to such a revolution. What was the October revolution, what indeed is the Communist party, but a miracle? No Menshevik could ever understand what is meant to be a member of such a party. The essential characteristic of this party is that it is bounded by no laws, it is always extending the realm of the possible until nothing becomes impossible. Nothing is inadmissible for it, nothing unrealizable. For such a party a true Bolshevik will readily cast out from his mind ideas in which he has believed for years. A true Bolshevik has submerged his personality in the collectivity, 'the party,' to such an extent that he can make the necessary effort to break away from his own opinions and convictions, and can honestly agree with the party—that is the test of a true Bolshevik." There could be no life for him, Piatakov continued, "outside of the ranks of the Party, and he would be ready to believe that black was white, and white was black, if the party required it. In order to become one with this great Party he would fuse himself with it, abandon his own personality, so that there was no particle left inside him which was not at one with the Party, did not belong to it." (Leonard Schapiro, *The Communist Party of the Soviet Union*, 1960, pp. 380 f.)

This confession of a Communist is remarkable in many ways and goes far to illuminate the relation between the idea system and the attitudes stemming from it. Meyer maintains that "a consciously held system of ideas plays a much greater part in the dynamics of the Communist personality than of the contemporary Western personality in general." (*The Moulding of Communists*, p. 49) In the above-mentioned report of a conversation, Piatakov spoke of the Party as "a miracle," and hailed it for not "being bounded" by any "laws," for "always extending the realm of the possible until nothing becomes impossible." We would do well to take the term "miracle" seriously. Piatakov had long accustomed himself to thinking of the world and of action in terms of "the laws of history" as Marxism defined them. According to historical materialism, no socialist revolution was possible in Russia until capitalism had fully developed and run its course to maturity. All the same, Lenin and the Communist Party had brought about what Piatakov believed to be a socialist revolution in Russia. Thus the idea system furnished Piatakov with his notions of "possibility" and "necessity," against which background the achievement of the Party appeared as a suspension of the "laws of history," as a "miracle." The idea system itself made Piatakov see the Party as something higher than the idea system, as above necessity, as the lord of possibilities, as something so much more real than all historical phases that no man could do better than to "become one" with this Party and to treat all his own ideas as of secondary importance. Piatakov sees in the Party a power above other powers, capable of making history in spite of history's own laws. Consequently he concludes that for him "there could be no life outside the

Party" because the Party is the ultimate center of life as cast in the mold of history.

Piatakov was probably right when he concluded that no Menshevik could understand him, and he might have said that most normal men would equally fail to grasp the inner tension between full acceptance of the Communist idea system and subordination of its particular propositions to the living entity of the Party. All the same, Piatakov's explanation of his typical attitude is unique only in that he spelled it out articulately, in a moment of great excitement. Among Communists, it is not unique but typical, as borne out by many biographical accounts or descriptions of Communist actions. A Communist does not look upon the Party primarily as an instrument for carrying into effect his political ideas, but rather as the sole island of *being*, in an environment of transience. The Communist Party is a collectivity composed of men and women who have such attitudes. Undoubtedly there have been other Marxists and even Leninists who put their ideas and purposes first and regarded the Party as an instrument, but these people either left the Party, were expelled, or denied the name of "Communists." It is a curious phenomenon that no one who quarreled with the Communist Party over the interpretation of the ideology has succeeded in attaching to his name or movement the attribute "Communist." The followers of Trotsky to this day are called "Trotskyites" rather than Communists, and the same is true of large groups, sometimes majorities within particular countries, e.g. Germany and the United States, which severed their connection with the Communist Party center in the Soviet Union. Thus the attitude toward the Party that has been characterized here is a central constitutive element of

Communism, and it differs radically from normal attitudes of citizens toward political parties. For a Communist, the Party can make mistakes, but since it is "advanced," i.e. ahead of all other people in its grasp of history and its lordship over material conditions, it still is more right than anyone else. No Communist is likely to regard the Party line with cynicism, because he is convinced that it is either the discovery of the correct path toward the future or else the expansion of hitherto limited possibilities.

The term "party" thus is a misnomer, for it fails to convey this peculiar relationship between members and the collectivity. Nor can one regard the term "conspiracy" as a suitable alternative, though Communists do operate conspiratorially even when they enjoy the fullest license granted them by a permissive liberalism. Our language has not coined a word to designate a collectivity which, though a tiny majority, claims to be the whole; which, though based on an ideology, asserts its standing above the ideology; which must deny and annihilate all loyalties other than to itself and imply the total submission of the entire human personality. In Communist-controlled countries public thanks are offered to "the Party" for every benefit or success, in the way in which people normally offer thanks to God for the harvest, or for having safely emerged from a danger. At the same time, the Communist Party does not envisage the incorporation of the majority of men into its community but seeks to attach them to its purposes by means of what it terms "support." Indeed, the term "attaching to the Party" is characteristic of ideological language dealing with large parts of the population, the proletariat, the peasantry, and others. The idea behind this denies a whole of which the Communist Party would see itself, even provisionally, as a part and suggests once again the total inadequacy of the word "party" for this phenomenon. Because of his total submission to the Party, the Communist will always be alienated from his fellow citizens and fellow men.

In judging this phenomenon and its durability one must not forget that the Party is composed of men and women who, fully knowing the ideology and also the total claim of the Party on its members, opted to join it. What is more, those who remain in the Party, and particularly those who rise in it to top rank, must have opted again and again, for the Party and against their own ideas, their consciences, and even their personalities. A Communist is bound to experience countless conflicts in his soul and his mind, brought about by his Party membership, and if he remains a member and is successful at it, it means that he has many times resolved these conflicts in favor of the Party. The scars which every Communist bears of these inner fights are what make him a Communist. Those who in wrestling with their consciences do not manage to come out on top fall by the wayside. Again, the records are full of instances of both kinds, one of the most impressive being related by Frank S. Meyer, who personally witnessed it. It was the case of a homosexual who, after a long career in the Party, was told at one point to break with his deviation within forty-eight hours or quit the Party. He chose submission and paid the painful price.

Although other typical Communist attitudes can be said to flow from the two basic ones already mentioned, it is not superfluous to point out two separately.

A Polarized World

Communists always see the world polarized. Marx
spoke of two, and only two, classes between whom the
decisive struggle is being waged. Engels divided all philosophy into two "camps." Lenin taught that "the only
choice is either bourgeois or socialist ideology. There is no
middle course (for humanity has not created a 'third'
ideology . . .) . . ."Later he arranged international politics
as a division between two great groups, the imperialist
countries and their enemies. In other words, for a Communist, mankind consists of two kinds, of which one does and
the other does not deserve to live. In this respect the
Communist attitude is first cousin to that of the Nazis'
distinction between human and subhuman beings. The
yardstick of value is either "support for the Party" or
"progressive vs. reactionary."

The second is a criterion related to the Communist's
orientation in time, already mentioned, and his dwelling in
the future rather than the present. The former presupposes
the Party as the only present force that is wholly justified
and thus implicitly "good," whereas all its opponents are
just as implicitly evil or frightfully mistaken. Everything in
the world is split into two, inevitably locked in struggle.
There are two classes contending in the class struggle:
bourgeoisie and proletariat; two mental orientations:
progressive and reactionary; two kinds of nations: imperialist and "peace-loving"; two kinds of wars: "imperialist"
and revolutionary; and similarly, two kinds of laws,
sciences, arts, and so on.

The Communists frequently do speak of "third forces,"
which they call "in-between," and which enable them to

account for many facts of life that otherwise would contradict their polarization. The "in-between" elements, however, are "third" only temporarily. For a while they may be neutral; ultimately, they can only be "really revolutionary" or—"vacillating," "petty-bourgeois," "unreliable," and "treacherous." Everything tends to line up in one great worldwide, historic clash, and those who now appear neutral cannot in the long run remain so. All the same, the existence of "neutral" forces, or elements that can effectively be "neutralized," plays an important role in Communist strategy. Still, Communists cannot help seeing even the most neutral or uncommitted group as eventually coming down on one or the other side, and will regard it as an ultimate element of "support" for the Party or else as an existential enemy. Compromise therefore does not belong to the mental world of the Communist, in the sense that he can see any viable ground between the two "camps." Compromise as a strategy is one of his revolutionary obligations, enjoined by Lenin himself, but this does not qualify the polarized picture of the world. He who steps out of the Communist camp has only one place to go: he invariably steps into the camp of the enemy. There is no difference between withdrawal from the Communist cause and betrayal.

Ubiquitous suspicion is a characteristic attitude accompanying the polarized view of the world. It has something to do with the Communist disdain for subjective intentions. A person may subjectively intend to be a revolutionary, but by virtue of ideologically incorrect attitudes, he may nevertheless "objectively" support the bourgeoisie; thus supporters or helpers of the enemy may always be present even within the Party. Lenin taught Communists

to distinguish themselves as "conscious," i.e. motivated by
their knowledge of the future, from the masses who are
"spontaneous," i.e. swayed by their interests in the present. Only "consciousness" is revolutionary, while "spontaneity" is reactionary. Now ordinary people are invariably "spontaneous," even under a Communist regime, and
thus the Communists feel themselves at all times "surrounded" by nefarious influences. An attitude of ceaseless
watchfulness is thus required; the Communists endeavor
at all times to keep themselves uncontaminated from a
surrounding world with which they have no community of
value or principle. In every dissent the Communist smells
the odor of bourgeois reaction; every trace of interest that
is not identified with the Party appears to him to be residue
of former ruling-class mentality. Everyone and everything
deserves distrust. Good standing can be earned only by
tireless loyalty to the Party and it can never be securely
enjoyed. Thus, to a Communist there is no such thing as
confidence in another person based on knowledge of that
person's character. The enemy is believed always to be
disguised and always needs to be "unmasked." The Communist struggle is protracted, sometimes felt to be unend-
ing, and it is the life that a Communist has elected. No
amount of goodwill or friendliness can overcome this self-
willed alienation of Communists from their fellow beings,
for the Communist ideology has invalidated all goodwill or
friendliness as "bourgeois illusion," in view of the basic
fact of the class struggle. In the same way, the Communists' venture into cooperation with the class enemy is
never based on the acceptance of the other side in good
faith but on the premise of the continuing struggle in

which it is sometimes expedient to cooperate in order to destroy the enemy's bastions from within.

Peaceless Struggle

The Communist view of the struggle as a protracted condition has already been mentioned. It may not be superfluous to point out that the Communists differ from normal people in their attitude toward conflict and struggle. For people in normal circumstances conflict is an interruption of life, something to be attended to and terminated as speedily as possible. For the Communist, struggle is the characteristic of the entire historical epoch in which he lives. As far as his own life is concerned, he has accepted struggle as its main purpose, leaving the fruits of the struggle to his children or possibly his grandchildren. Militancy is the attitude which he expects to dominate his every moment and action. Since he looks on struggle as a condition rather than a campaign or crusade, something which precisely is "protracted" rather than dramatic, everything in life is viewed in terms of struggle. One cannot push the struggle to an abrupt victorious conclusion; its duration is indefinite, and no spectacular victory will crown it. One day, says the Communist, "we will awake and it will be over." Here lies the explanation of the typical Communist "toughness." Defeats and setbacks cannot daunt a mind that considers the future already his. The present is uncertain, to be sure, an "entire historical era, replete with civil wars and external conflicts, with persistent organizational work and economic construction, with advances and retreats, victories and defeats."

One should note how in this characterization from Stalin's pen "economic construction" and "organizational work" are sandwiched in between "civil wars and external conflicts," and "victories and defeats." "Economic construction," as well as science, art, entertainment, and even sports all have meaning only through the struggle, and as means of struggle. Mankind has not yet arrived at its future home; there is no order to be enjoyed, no good time to be savored. The good time is still to come, and the Party's total triumph is its threshold. Khrushchev's "We shall bury you!" was meant, not as a declaration of intent but as a factual statement, the perspective in which Communists see all things in life. It is impossible for a Communist to look on any task or problem in isolation from this perspective of struggle. To do so would mean to embrace an attitude of "bourgeois objectivity" which has already been "unmasked" as an illusion. He may, of course, acknowledge that in economics cost-accounting is a problem that must be solved, that productivity in agriculture has its own requirements, that a legal system is governed by its own logic. If he is a good manager or administrator, he will be able to isolate these intrinsic features, but he would not be a Communist if he could ever look at such problems and not also view them as elements in th Communist strategy. In this sense Lenin long ago laid down the maxim that Communists may take an interest in social reforms but not for their own sake, rather only as means to advance the strategic position.

Much is being made at present of the thesis that Communists are motivated only by a desire for power and use the ideology as an instrument to gain and secure power positions. The thesis is a half truth. It is true that Communists distinguish themselves from so-called "utopians" by insisting that the perfect society cannot be "made" but can emerge only from "conditions," and that the prime condition to be met is the Party's total victory over the class enemy and its every legacy. This means that Communism concentrates wholly on the goal of total power, and that the long road to the future appears in this perspective as that of a power struggle carried on in all relations of human life. Whatever the Communist Party undertakes aims directly or indirectly at increasing its power, strengthening its organization, preparing conditions for new advances. This much of the thesis is true. The untruth stems from a projection of a concept of "power" that would be entertained by normal people in a normal society, into the Communist world. Someone aspiring to the Presidency of the United States desires power, meaning that he would like to lead others, issue commands, begin and direct the public actions of this country, and enter into the annals of history with a title to fame. It is very much of a personal ambition, and thus those who for some reason or other are disappointed in their hopes can be compensated, either by other positions of prominence, or by opportunities to get rich, or by other kinds of fame. Some personal ambitions must doubtlessly also move individual Communists. The collectivity of the Party, however, cannot be understood as a society for the joint attainment of personal ambitions. It is a society for the increase of power that has an ideological quality. Had Communist leaders wanted nothing more than to stand high among their fellow Russians, surely Stalin would have identified himself with the peasantry that constituted the overwhelming majority of the Russian people. Instead, he launched on a policy that implied a declaration of war against the peasantry, brought the entire Party to the brink of disaster, resulted in a permanent weakness in agriculture, and retarded the entire economic development of Russia. If one were to attribute Stalin's decision to a misjudgment which he afterwards had reason to regret, one would be hard put to explain how the Chinese Communists, in full knowledge of the Russian difficulties from collectivization, decided to tread the same path as late as 1956. The Communist quest for power, in quantitative terms, is indeed unlimited, but qualitatively speaking, no Communist would be satisfied with the kind of power enjoyed, let us say, by a Franklin D. Roosevelt or a Charles de Gaulle. As Communists increase their power and lay the foundations for further and tighter controls, they desire power capable of changing men and their relations in a specific direction. Power has its own logic, its inherent requirements, but to Communists these appear, albeit with great clarity, only as either aids or impediments in regard to their ideological purpose. Power interests them only as that which they believe can bend stubborn human realities to their ideological image.

CHAPTER 3

Irrationality in Communist Theory and Practice

Irrationality in Governments?

Communists characterized in terms of their ideology may be one thing, but are not Communists when ruling a country quite another? A party in opposition or on its way to power might well indulge in all kinds of irrational moods or dreams which the responsibility of governing might disperse. On such premises we incline to assume that governments of complex societies could not operate except rationally, their rationality being prescribed by the logic of management, judicial administration, or diplomacy. It is this assumption that caused Neville Chamberlain to wager that Hitler's wildness was but a façade behind which he was sure to find an old-fashioned nationalism limited to the desire to see all Germans united within one country. On this premise he proceeded to satisfy Hitler's excessive but basically rational demands, believing that by doing so he had bought "peace in our time." It soon became manifest that Hitler's Munich demands were not identical with his goals, that his expansionism sprang from irrational sources and thus admitted of no concrete limits, nor could they be satisfied by concrete concessions. This experience has caused many thoughtful people to revise their ideas and to take into consideration the possibility of irrationally motivated governments. Unfortunately, this revision is often cut short by a resolve to regard Hitler as a unique case that should be explained in terms of either a psychopathic personality or a psychopathic national character. John Plamenatz, for instance, concludes his book, *German Marxism and Russian Communism* (Harper Torchbook, 1965), with this sigh of relief: "Let us at least thank God that Hitler is dead, and that the dictators we have now to deal with are sane."

Plamenatz is referring to Communist leaders, i.e., not any variety of dictators but rather totalitarian rulers. The question whether totalitarian rule warrants the attribute of sanity is not the same as whether a particular ruler suffers from some kind of mental derangement. Rather, it is the question of the relationship between a particular kind of ruling body, one that is motivated by an ideological drive for total power, and its subject people. Our yardstick of judgment, or standard of "normalcy," in this respect is what we call "legitimate government," a body of rulers holding office by an acknowledged title to authority. In the nature of things, legitimation can be derived only from somebody or something higher than the governing body itself, whether this be God, the people, a higher law, or historical tradition. A government claiming legitimacy acknowledges a higher source of its authority to which it submits the validity of its title. We also gauge the legitimacy of government by another test, the end of its actions. Implicit in the concept of government is the purpose of the common good, the order, safety, and welfare of the community and its members. The government, while in a position of command, legitimizes itself by serving the common good. The *terminus ad quem* of this service is living men and women, as they are by virtue of their personalities, and the customs and habits that constitute their common patrimony. These given human beings and patterns of living constitute a limit for government. We refer to this limitation in many ways, as when we speak of the "inviolability" of the human person, or of government as being for the people rather than people for the government, or of the "dignity of man." These one might call ontological limits of government, which express themselves in moral inhibitions. Besides these, however, the same human premises limit governments in a political way. Every political action is a strand in a web of other actions, relationships, and institutions which are affected by it and affect it in turn, and thereby circumscribe the limits of what "is possible." In this sense, action based on pure principle is not only inhuman but also impolitic and can be likened to a person pursuing some objective as if he were alone in the world. Political rationality is based on acceptance of the limitation of all politics by the historical matrix, the natures of men and women, their habits and customs, and spontaneous human aspirations. Measured by such standards, Communist regimes cannot and do not claim legitimacy.

The Non-Legitimacy of Communist Regimes

The crucial fact is that the Communist Party regards itself not as within the political order but as above it. It neither claims nor accepts title to authority validated by anything above itself, because it acknowledges nobody and nothing above itself. It rejects God and has sworn irreconcilable hostility to the religions held among Russians. The notion of a higher law is to Communists nothing but "bourgeois prejudice." The Communists claim a special morality geared to the Party's interests. As for the state, not only do the Communists deny any state continuity in Russia, but they have also demoted the state to the role of a mere instrument through which the Party is to realize its will. They call it one of the "transmission belts," the organizations through which a numerically small Party can manipulate vast masses into supporting its, the Party's, enterprise. These "transmission belts" are organizations called into existence by natural or spontaneous needs and desires of people rather than by Communist doctrine, so that Communists pursue their sectarian purposes in a concealed fashion, by covertly using institutions which people are naturally driven to establish and join. The state, too, is a natural association of humans which responds to a basic and general need for order and thus is capable of attracting loyalties, regardless of who or what controls it at the top. The Communists, however, do not look on the state in a spirit of loyalty because they do not think of themselves as parts of the state. On the one hand, the state in their doctrine figures only as a temporary phenomenon, bound to disappear in the future. On the other, their own authority is not that of a part of the political system but rather that of an enterprise engaged in changing the world. It is they who prescribe norms to the state, not the state to them. The word "party" thus does not properly apply to the Communist organization which rather claims to be the whole, the whole of meaning, the whole of order, the whole of power, the whole of law. With regard to this whole, the state figures as but a part, one of the several instruments at the Party's disposal. Besides the state, there are other "transmission belts," and the Khrushchevian devolution of political functions onto "social organizations" such as the trade unions and the Komsomols shows that the Party in a pinch can use transmission belts other than the state. Nor are the the people a source of authority in Communist eyes. The Program of the CPSU of 1961 speaks of the relations between the Party and the people as those between teacher and pupil. The people are thus cast in a role of immaturity and the Party in that of the exclusive possessor of truth and wisdom. "The Party is the brain, the honor, and the conscience of our epoch, of the Soviet people." In such a relation any deference to the people is inconceivable. The Party, far from acknowledging "the people" as the source of its authority, usurps a position above the people from which it judges and shapes the people. Thus neither God nor law, nor state, nor people, nor tradition can bestow title of authority on the Party. In view of all known possibilities of legitimation, the Party's rule is without legitimacy. Bertram Wolfe drives home this point by reminding us of the important distinction in 1917, between the "Provisional Government," which indicated through its name that it was no more than a caretaker pending the meeting of an all-Russian Constituent Assembly, and the Communists who dispersed the duly elected Constituent Assembly, thereby making a deliberate choice against legitimacy (*An Ideology in Power*, 1969).

What does it mean when the ruling group in a country

lacks legitimacy? In such a situation, rulers and ruled do
not share the rationale of political power. The rulers have
decided that their rule does not serve the usual purposes
of a government except as a means to an end, and that end
is one which they embrace exclusively as a group, apart
from the members of the society. One might speculate
whether the Communist belief in a future society of perfection could not serve as a legitimacy of sorts, since it is this
goal which attracts members to the Communist Party and
justifies, in their eyes, all the hardships and harshnesses of
the present struggle. A future goal, however, in its very
nature denies the dedication of the rulers to the purpose
of a normal government, which is the common good of the
living generation of actual people. The Party's struggle for
a mythical future must thus remain an exclusive cause of
loyalty and divisive justification, valid only for those who
are adepts of the Communist ideology, and incapable of
legitimizing the Communist rule over the vast numbers of
people who are not Communist and who will not benefit
from the Communist-envisioned future even if it should
come to pass. The position of the Party in power is thus
comparable to that of a regime of military occupation.
That comparison has in fact been made regarding the Nazi
Party which also ruled in order to attain the goals of an
ideological enterprise to change the world. In the memoirs
of Werner Bergengruen *(Schreibtischerinnerungen)* we
find the following observation: "Sometimes it was almost
as if the men of the party and its affiliated bodies were
members of an army of invasion or occupation who had
insufficient command of the language of the country they
had conquered and in consequence learned little of the

conversations and thoughts of the suppressed natives." If the rulers are not legitimate, they rule as if they were strangers.

Legitimacy engenders mutual confidence and public faith, confidence in the ruled that the common good is the rulers' concern. When legitimacy is absent, and public faith is missing, the rulers are necessarily fearful and suspicious. Not only the slightest criticism but even indifference or mere lukewarm support serves them as indication of a hidden hostility. The assumption that among their own people there are always "enemies" is typical of totalitarian regimes who wield power only in order to realize their ideological goals. No "party" which claims to be above the people, the state, and the tradition, and which denies God and a higher law and follows a morality of its own, can ever hope to escape this condition—being as if at war with members of its own society. For such a party does not belong. It rules only to remake people into something they do not want to be. It cannot assume that its commands are willingly received because the legitimacy of its rule is accepted on general grounds. Thus the rationale of its commands is not necessarily understood, and, if understood, not necessarily credited with good faith. A number of Soviet writers, and others who have lived in Russia, have compared life in Russia with life in a forced labor camp, the characteristic of which is total power brutally enforced, in a system which as a whole makes no sense and does not serve the ordinary purposes of the good life. Nobody feels that the system as a whole concerns *him*, except those whose thinking is molded entirely in terms of five-year plans, production quotas, and labor

norms, i.e. those who have made the ideological aspirations of the Party their own. Inefficiency necessarily attends a system which everybody disowns, again the only
exception being those who regard the system as the means
to their ideological ends.

Political Irrationality and Total Power

How, then, do Communists retain power? Essentially in
two ways: by isolating each individual person before the
collectivity, and by manipulating people into supporting
the Party in spite of themselves. The isolation proceeds
both institutionally and psychologically. With regard to
institutions, the Party seeks to eliminate every organization that arises from the spontaneous activity or volition
of people, any institution that is the people's own in the
sense that they have originated it and maintain it. Rather,
the Party strives to have every single institution depend on
its, the Party's, initiative, direction, and regulation. No
chess club, no cultural association, no sports establishment
can be formed without the Party; no apartment house can
exist without a Party supervisor; no grouping of people is
allowed to operate in its own way. Spontaneity is suspect,
and "consciousness" is the Party's monopoly. Psychologically, the Party causes particular individuals to confront
the collectivity in a way that presupposes the individual's
condemnation even before he is indicted. The individual
is always made to feel selfish and alone, the collectivity is
made to appear righteous and powerful. More important,
however, are the manipulative devices. Every activity of
men, coming as it does from their natural needs, natural
abilities, and natural aspirations, is diverted to serve the

Party's strategic purposes. Hans Buchheim points out that "the Communists consider a good movie, an athletic victory, a scientific discovery, or a technical invention to be testimony of the resolve to build socialism. A foreign visitor in Moscow cannot express his admiration for the Kremlin's old works of art or his gratitude for the helpfulness of his guide without having his words interpreted as an acknowledgement of Communism or a demonstration in favor of 'peace'." (*Totalitarian Rule, Its Nature and Characteristics,* 1968) The need of a man to clothe himself and his family is used by means of cunningly arranged prices, to force him and his wife to a maximum of work; the desire for promotion becomes a main lever in the Party's control over men; the habit of reading enables the government to indoctrinate millions by its monopoly of all printing and publication. The whole system is a vast exploitation of the needs and necessities of people, as well as of their spontaneous activities, for political purposes not intended by them. The Communists who indict capitalism for economic exploitation have not abolished that kind of exploitation but rather compounded it with political exploitation that is not confined to workers but includes all people and everything that people do. Not merely the labor, but also the leisure of people is subject to exploitation, and exploitation is the basis not merely of the formation of capital but also of the augmentation of totalitarian power.

In this context, a special word needs to be said about nationalism. A Communist Party ruling Russia as if it were alien could never hope to wage a successful war with the help of the Russian people. Thus in World War II, which Stalin called the Great Patriotic War, Russian nationalism was activated, the heroes of Russian history were dusted off, patriotic devotion to the homeland was made to appear the sole motive of the Communist leaders and thus a duty which leaders and the Russian people shared. Nationalism and patriotism are natural emotions not without moral value, the stronger the more a people remembers its public past. As long as a people continues in existence, can think back to the days of its fathers, remains conscious of sharing language, culture, and a common way of life, nationalism and patriotism will always be present. They can be exploited just as much as a man's devotion to his family, need to work, and desire for advancement. Particularly a regime lacking legitimacy would find the exploitation of nationalism the easiest way to secure support from a vast population among which it suspects many enemies. Such exploitation, however, will have a hollow ring unless the country is, or can be made to appear, threatened by external enemies. Totalitarian regimes cannot maintain themselves in the long run without the myth of a mortal enemy, because the exploitation of nationalism is their sole means of coming close to something resembling legitimacy. When national existence as such seems threatened, nobody asks whether the nation's leaders have a title to command, because to have a commander is more important than to have a legitimate commander. Legitimacy is a peacetime issue: totalitarianisms therefore can never allow wartime to come to an end. "Peace" may be their slogan, but war is their political sustenance.

In so far as Communists wield power of government, their relationship to their subjects is not that between government and governed in the normal sense. In other words, it is a mistake to look upon Communist regimes as governments. The Greek political philosophers made a significant distinction between government and tyranny, calling government an exercise of public power that served the ends of government and tyranny one that served other ends which appeared as perversions of politics, or as irrationality in public affairs. They assumed that the source of this irrationality was the character of the tyrant, whom they saw as being enslaved to base passions and incapable of public service. In the case of modern totalitarian movements, however, irrationality stems from their ideologies, which cause a body of men and women, the members of the Party, to shut themselves off from their fellow men, to look upon themselves as beings of a special category and on their whole movement as something justified beyond normal good and evil. Such movements have existed before Fascism, Nazism, and Communism, but never on such a large scale and never in possession of such formidable power resources. In modern times, ideologies creating essentially irrational assumptions about reality have arisen since the end of the eighteenth century and particularly in the middle of the nineteenth century. Robert Musil, the modern Austrian novelist, has brilliantly analyzed the kind of thinking typical of such men and women in his novel, *The Man Without Qualities*. What he calls "the sickness of our time" is a willingness to live in a world spun out of arbitrary and wishful ideas spun out apart from the reality of experience. People who give themselves to such ideas disdain, so Musil says, "real possibilities" in order to speculate about "possible realities," or, as Charles Williams puts it, strain to "adapt the world to their idea of a world." They sever in their minds their link with reality as it is, and thus fall into a kind of restless excitement looking for ever newer dream shores. They begin to live in what Musil calls a "Second Reality," a web of willful notions opposed to experience which they come to accept as if they actually were reality.

The Communists constitute one of the "Second Reality" groups in our time. In the real world, men live in the necessity of having to make decisions toward an essentially unknown future. In the Communists' dream world, however, the future appears as essentially known, so that the present must be adapted to that pre-known future; Communists look upon the future as more real than the present, and as the ultimate and highest justification of whatever they are doing. One may say that the Communists have made their home in the future instead of living in the present. This point of view is basically irrational. History as a whole is not given, it has not yet happened, so that the future is not a datum but rather a task. He who claims foreknowledge of the future abandons the position of man whose decisions have to be made precisely with a view to an unknown future. Instead, he adopts the point of view of a being beyond time to whom all of history, the future as well as the past, is ever present. "Communists should know that, at all events, the future belongs to them," said Lenin.

This manner of thinking, however, has vast consequences for their present relationships and actions. As the future is to them that which alone justifies their actions, the present is not a dimension in which to live but a transition, to be left as soon as possible. They do not consider themselves at home in this world of the present. Their alienation in the present world separates them from all those who do live in the present. Communists, who regard themselves as the army of the goddess of the future, look upon themselves as a separate group, an elite group, distinguished among all others by their knowledge of what is yet hidden from ordinary men. Lenin repeatedly emphasized the virtue of "independent thinking," by which he meant not so much reliance on one's critical faculties, as a type of thought that manages to detach itself from all influences of the present and molds itself entirely on the foreknown future. This is the meaning of Lenin's notion of "consciousness," or equally that of his "revolutionary ideology," or "advanced theory." All of these are "godwords" among Communists. The chief result of this thinking is that the Communists fail to accept for themselves what is commonly called the "human condition." Someone who denies that he is living in the human condition must be, according to Aristotle, either a god or a beast. In the second book of the *Republic*, Plato relates the legend of one who felt free to commit a series of atrocious crimes because he had found a ring that made him invisible among men. Plato tells this story as having occurred in a dream, or, in other words, belonging to a dream world. The real world is one in which man lives among fellow men and is bound by his relations with them. Martin Buber insists that the commandment "Love they neighbor as thyself" should be translated: "Love thy neighbor as one like thyself." These are a few of the repeated insistences of great thinkers that human rationality begins with the acceptance of the common condition in which all men find themselves. The Communists, making a sharp and essential distinction between those who possess knowledge of the future and all the rest of men, basically reject the community of the human condition.

The Closed Mind of Ideologists

Irrationality also prevails in the Communist attitude toward its own ideology. Communists call Marxism-Leninism a "science," look on their operations as "scientific" and on their ultimate goal as the complete conscious control of nature and society by men. That, however, is not the whole story . If it were, one might accuse the Communists merely of an excessive rationalism, rather than of irrationality. Any science is based.on critical examination and reexamination. The Communists, however, have put the main ideas of Marx and Lenin beyond any examination whatsoever. Questioning them is forbidden, and this prohibition is surrounded by powerful sanctions. Dogmatism and science belong to different realms, but the Communists believe they can be scientific when they treat the main propositions of their vaunted science as dogmas. To be sure, their ideology has changed many times, but each change has been wrought tortuously, bending old dogmas into new shapes or overlaying them with new interpretations while pretending that they are still the same. On the other hand, the "science" of Marxism–Leninism has capsuled itself off against any contradictory facts. When history belied Marx's "law" of a gradually worsening misery of the proletariat, and the real wages of labor did not fall but rose, Lenin claimed that "imperialism" had "bribed" its working class and shifted the worst exploitation to the overseas colonies. When Lenin himself stated that imperialism would not last if the capitalist countries could solve their problem of agriculture and subsequently this problem was solved, the Communists simply dropped the talk of "imperialism" and began the talk about "neoimperialism."

One can also find a kind of irrational manipulation of the ideology which seems to make perfect sense to Communists. The whole Communist movement is founded on the prediction of the coming socialist society, the "realm of freedom." In Communist writings, especially in Marx and Engels, it appears that that end would be attained once private ownership of the means of production was abolished. That kind of private property was abolished in Russia half a century ago, and in China in 1949. Since the "realm of freedom" is not yet in sight, the Communists have extended again and again the "period of transition from capitalism to socialism." That period was first divided by Marx into a "lower" phase and a "higher" phase, later named "socialism" and "Communism." Since then the Communists have added many subdivisions to these two: The "beginning of the construction of socialism," the "construction of socialism," the "completion of the construction of socialism," the preparation for the "beginning of the construction of Communism," and recently they have begun to distinguish between a "lower" and a "mature" Communism. In other words, they are engaged in endlessly extending the period of expection—and struggle —and pushing back the consummation of the movement to a more and more remote future.

The world of the ideologist is thus enclosed in its own terms, a complete system that bears only remote resemblance to the fact of experience. The ideological mind, moving around in terms of this system, however, has an answer for every question. James Burnham, in his *Suicide of the West*, painted an apt portrait of the irrational ideologist:

A convinced believer in the anti-Semitic ideology tells
me that the Bolshevik revolution is a Jewish plot. I point
out to him that the revolution was led to its first major
victory by a non-Jew, Lenin. He then explains that Lenin
was the pawn of Trotsky, Radek, Kamenev, Zinoviev, and
other Jews who were in the Bolshevik High Command. I
remind him that Lenin's successor as leader of the revolution, the non-Jew Stalin, killed off all those Jews; and that
Stalin has been followed by the non-Jew Khrushchev, under whose rule there have been notable revivals of anti-
Semitic attitudes and conduct. He then informs me that
the seeming Soviet anti-Semitism is only a fraud invented
by the Jewish press, and that Stalin and Khrushchev are
really Jews whose names have been changed, with a total
substitution of forged records. Suppose I am able to present documents that even he will have to admit show this
to be impossible? He is still unmoved. He tells me that the
real Jewish center that controls the revolution and the
entire world conspiracy is not in Russia anyway, but in
Antwerp, Tel Aviv, Lhasa, New York or somewhere, and
that it has deliberately eliminated the Jews from the public
officialdom in the Bolshevik countries in order to conceal
its hand and deceive the world about what is going on.
Q.E.D.

This kind of distortion of the ideologist's sense of reality
is what dooms the ideologist to perpetual conflict with the
world. This is true of all ideologies, but more particularly
of the Communist ideology, which explicitly maintains
that the road to its mythical goal is by way of an "irreconcilable struggle," a "period of transition" full of overt and
covert fighting, a political regime defined as "the organization not of order but the organization of war."

Plato described political irrationality as stemming from
the ascendancy of dark and "unlawful" passions over the

soul's element of reason. In this sense he failed to describe the irrationality of totalitarianism which springs not from mere lusts. All the same, one can speak of a passion, not the self-seeking passion of Plato's tyrant but rather a passion to bend the reality of being to that image of the Second Reality which is an arbitrary creation of the mind. What one can see in the forces of Nazism and Communism is an *ideological passion*, a force positing itself in a permanent quarrel with the reality of experience, and in this commitment to conflict remaining endemically impotent to achieve peace and order. Ideological passion may be more dangerous than self-seeking passion, for its addicts feel absolved from the charge of petty selfishness. It is not their personal gratification they are seeking but the enactment of the ideological vision that stands over against them like something majestically demanding allegiance and devotion. E. Winance, in *The Communist Persuasion*, describes the supreme emotional and intellectual pressure under which his Chinese Communist captors put him, a pressure operating essentially with arguments against egotism and for selfless devotion to the Revolution. In this sense, each Communist is subordinating his own self to the cause and this fact causes many to look on Communism as something wholly noble and admirable. Not all dedication, however, can be called good. Communists are wholly devoted to a Second Reality which can never be accepted as the common good and therefore always gives rise to alienation and oppression.

Modern political science has succeeded in throwing a great deal of light on ideological movements when it discovered the similarity between modern ideologies and the various religious movements of Antiquity known as

Gnosticism. On the basis of many studies probing this phenomenon, Eric Voegelin (*Science, Politics, and Gnosticism,* 1968), has analyzed "such movements as progressivism, positivism, Marxism, psychoanalysis, communism, fascism, and national socialism," finding that they resemble Gnosticism in the following features:

1. The Gnostic is dissatisfied with his situation.

2 . He attributes the evils of the situation to the fact that the world is intrinsically badly organized. This is remarkable, for one can also assume that the order of being is good and that we human beings are inadequate. But the Gnostics are not inclined to assume any blame for the situation.

3. The Gnostic believes that salvation from the evils of the world is possible.

4. He also believes that this salvation will occur through an historical process: the world will change from wretched to good. This is also remarkable, for Christians assume that the world will not change essentially throughout history and that salvation will come to man through grace in death.

5. Here we come to the crux of the matter: The Gnostic believes that salvation can be attained through an historical, human effort in the sociopolitical realm.

6. The Gnostic sees the key to this in his correct knowledge of the formula for historical salvation. He himself is ready to proclaim this knowledge and head the salvational enterprise.

In other words, the characteristic of the totalitarian movements is their belief that politics can save man, as a result of which politics becomes religion, as Camus put it.

It seems that a radical polarization between a world deemed totally and hopelessly evil and a redeeming political force has a powerful emotional and intellectual appeal. Once it has taken hold of a person, common sense and reason drop out of reach and traditional loyalties crumble. In a tightly knit company of like-minded adepts, such persons can develop devastating energy, energy which is dissolvent rather than constructive. As we have seen, this mentality also prevents such movements from establishing governments. All they can attain is regimes. For the same reason, there is no such thing as a totalitarian form of government: there are only regimes of totalitarian movements. Since they occupy the seats of government, people are apt to mistake them for normal government and to treat with them on the basis of supposedly common political assumptions. The basic motivation of totalitarianism, as Buchheim has pointed out, is nonpolitical because it is nongovernmental. An ideological group in control of a nation will, of course, look after that nation's power requirements, for the nation is the main instrument of its strategy. In that sense, political and nonpolitical motivations may merge for a while. The result, however, can never be "politics as usual," but always must be a perversion of political relationships.

CHAPTER 4

The Evolution
of Communism

It is only natural that the world should speculate on the direction in which Communism is likely to evolve. The entire phenomenon is so strange and alien that one cannot imagine it as lasting. Those who, in a defeatist mood, have resigned themselves to the notion that Communism "is here to stay" also insist that they mean a Communism shorn of its revolutionary features. They join with others in celebrating the passing of the ideology, that enigmatic and disturbing source of irrational conduct. The Western world inclines to the belief that there will be a happy ending, meaning that the incitement to revolutionary expansionism will first weaken and then die without having first brought the world to a nuclear catastrophe.

Fallacious Models of Comparison

While such wishful thinking may be a luxury which sober men cannot afford, some ideas on the evolution of Communism are obviously required. The point, then, is to see that they move within the limits of real possibilities rather than in the fiction of possible realities. Unfortunately, even experts in this field often speculate in an uncritical manner. In the first place, some of them apply to Soviet development the model of European history in the 17th and 18th centuries, with its movement from absolutism to freedom, a movement that is often confused with the necessity of history as a whole. Unfortunately, the historical precedent is both ambiguous and irrelevant. Ambiguous, because one can find at least three ways in which absolutism in Europe developed: a) English absolutism, facing a united front of nobility and third estate, was gradually mitigated in a series of conflicts out of which grew the unwritten constitution and the rights of Englishmen. b) French absolutism, leaning on the third estate, battered down the power of the nobility and steadily increased the strength of the central government, so that when the violent explosion of the French Revolution brought the *ancien régime* to an end, the succeeding governments retained strongly centralized power. c) Austria, Prussia, and other countries developed "enlightened" despotism: government for but not by the people, government dedicated to welfare but not liberty. Thus only the English precedent constitutes an "evolution" towards freedom. What is more, the entire precedent of absolutism fails to apply to Communism, for the former grew historically under legitimate dynasties which shared their peoples' religion and morality, while Communism is neither traditional nor legitimate, nor even a type of government, but rather an organized political enterprise and conceives of itself as a stranger in its present environment.

Another precedent by which some experts often gauge

the path of Communism is the French Revolution. Again, the precedent itself is misunderstood, and also does not fit Communism. Within six years, the French Revolution had run the cycle from insurrection to representative govern-ment to terror to utilitarian administration. Hence people draw from it the comforting conclusion that "revolutions lose their *élan*," meaning that revolutionary intoxication lasts but a short while and then gives way to the normal motivations of statesmen. Actually, things did not happen this way in France. The ideological organizers of the Ter-ror remained ideologically intoxicated to their very end. They lost, not their "*élan*" but rather their heads, which were chopped off by nonideological elements who, after a Terror of relatively short duration, happened still to be alive and were lucky in bringing off a *coup*. Beyond that, the precedent of the French Revolution fails to apply to Communism, for the former was an impersonal and fre-quently spontaneous process whereas the latter is a single organized enterprise. Many groups had their share in the French Revolution, the people's spontaneity played no small role, the whole process resembled waves of feverish mass excitement that produced events, lifted and dropped groups and individuals, and could not be attributed as a whole to any one organization, will, or intelligence. The Russian equivalent of the French Revolution would then be the six months between the collapse of the autocracy and the Bolshevik takeover. From then on, however, the history of Russia merges into the history of the Commu-nist Party. If one wishes to learn about an *élan*, provided the term applies, it cannot be the result of a chaotic inter-play of revolutionary impulses, but must be something found within the organized and disciplined enterprise of the Party. In other words, whatever one may learn from the French Revolution has no bearing on the development of Soviet Communism.

One wonders whether there is any precedent in history that might shed light on Communism. After all, there has never been a similar combination of a semireligious idea system with a tightly knit organization for political action, not, at least, on the scale of Communism. Some comparisons come to mind, only to be immediately rejected. The Jesuits in the 17th century had quasi-military unity and discipline but their purpose was never mainly political, and the organization was not meant to assume overt control over peoples and countries. The Jacobins of the French Revolution had an ideological purpose similar to the Communists', but they never achieved a centrally directed unity and certainly no worldwide organization. Discipline, unity, capacity for political action, on the other hand, have often been achieved under ambitious rulers, none of whom, however, had ideological purposes. Then again, idea systems have drawn people into groups, but in most cases such groupings have remained intellectual or emotional without converting themselves into disciplined organizations. Even Mussolini's Fascism and Hitler's National Socialism differ from Communism, in that they centered much more in the personality of the leader than Communism, which centers in Marxist-Leninist ideology.

Communism, then, is a unique case, with an organization custom-built to fit the ideology, and the ideology made the constitutive principle of the organization. We do not know whether Fascism or Nazism could have survived the death of their original leaders. Communism has already demonstrated three times that it can sustain its unity under changing leadership. Thus there must be an *élan*—provided the term is suitable—inherent in the ideological

cohesion organized in the Party. Communist leaders have
sought total power as much or more than Hitler and Mussolini did, but the Party is not based on the leadership
principle so much as on ideological discipline, and it is the
latter which again and again produces leadership cul-
minating in a single person. Adherence to a common
ideology and unconditional subordination to the Party
leadership constitute a complex of two intertwined criteria
that make up the *élan* of Communism. There is an element
of ideological proposition in this: no person would be
recognized as a Communist who asserted that imperialism
was not bad, or who refused to believe in a future Communist society. At the same time, one cannot be a Communist
apart from the official political line adopted by the Party
leadership. When talking of the evolution of Communism,
we have to pay attention to this complex relationship between general ideas, political purpose, and organized
unity. Moreover, we have to see this entity in its position
of control of large nations, whose people are not its broth-
ers but its subjects. To some extent the history of the
Communist Party of the Soviet Union gives us certain
evidence regarding evolution. As regards the future, however, we cannot fall back on comforting historical antece-
dents but must try to put ourselves into the shoes of
Communists in Russia, and seek to know the trends of
their minds.

The Record of Party History

In the past, the unity of the Party has been achieved
repeatedly by the practice of "splitting," i.e. severing its
connection with elements that previously were parts of a

common entity but had developed ideologically incompatible notions. "Splitting" has worked in one of two directions: either the Communists withdrew from a group to which they belonged but no longer considered revolutionary, or they cast ideologically defective elements out from their own ranks. In any case, the spirit of compromise has been wholly alien to the Communist enterprise. Lenin's formula "better fewer, but better" is rooted in his early statement: "The *only choice* is either bourgeois or socialist ideology. There is no middle course (for humanity has not created a 'third' ideology . . .)." Accordingly, in any ideological difference, the Party has opted for separation. Two aspects of this record need to be noted particularly: on the one hand, no group excommunicated by the Party has been able effectively to claim that it represents Communism; on the other hand, both the terms in which these intra-Party fights were conducted and their results have been generally accepted by victors and losers alike. It is useful to remind oneself that the terms of these fights are reflected in the clichés used by both sides: the highest yardstick is "The Revolution," in relation to which there are charges of "betrayal," "counterrevolution," "reaction," and so on. Fears of a potential "restoration" are expressed. The worst charges are of being on the side of "imperialism," "fascism," or "the monopolists," "warmongers," or "racists." Even clichés referring to the rest of the world are commonly used by both sides: "vacillating," "petit-bourgeois," "unreliable," "treacherous." Such clichés reveal the perspectives within which and with regard to which the quarrels arise. Aristotle said that the rich and the poor are mentally crippled in that they have permanently distorted views of each other and see each other only as either rich or poor, but not as human beings. Similarly, not only Communists but also the victims of their ideological anathema never see human beings but only "revolutionaries" or "imperialists," "proletarian fighters" or "traitors to the Revolution." Each difference of opinion becomes a power struggle in which not only the Party itself but the Revolution and the fate of mankind are supposed to be at stake. If even the victims of Party purges give their assent to this stacked deck of cards, one must assume that still in the hour of direst personal danger they cannot escape the spell of an ideologically distorted world view. Here we have evidence of the overpowering intellectual and emotional commitment that has enabled the Party again and again to inflict terrible injury on its faithful without falling apart, to restore its own discipline and unity in fight after factional fight. What is more, the claim of the Party to represent a historically ordained destiny has been effective far beyond its ranks; even non-Marxists and non-Communists speak of the Party's cause as "The Revolution," as witnessed by Western speculations of what the precise meaning of "The Revolution" is and how mankind will be affected by it. There are astonishingly few people who have come to see the Party as an emperor without clothes. One recalls the scene in Whittaker Chambers' *Witness* where Chambers first visits Krivitsky, the defector from the GPU, in the latter's room. When Krivitsky opens with the probing question whether "the Party" has "become fascist," Chambers, after a period of silent agony, replies affirmatively, whereupon Krivitsky accepts him fully, for the sake of that agonized silence. As for the West, it seems to have accepted the Communists' claim to represent "The Revolution," partly by treating "The Revolution" as historically inevitable and thus "likely to stay," partly by trying to steal its appeal to the peoples of the world and to assert that America is revolutionary, too. In other words, the Party's self-styled "world historical mission" has found well-nigh universal recognition. Those very few who have dared to withhold their assent from this claim have, in doing so, deliberately chosen despair, as witness Pasternak, or Whittaker Chambers, who stated that he had knowingly "chosen the losing side." Their lot can be likened to that of the existentialists who, in denouncing God, consciously embrace absurdity—heroes of hopelessness.

The Force of External Realities

How about the Party's evolution in the face of external obstacles or difficulties? Let us remember that there is a structural difference between the anonymous process of the French Revolution and the organized unity of the Communist Party. Regarding the former, essentially a phenomenon of mass psychology, it is pertinent to look for "laws" of fatigue or mortality. Regarding the Party, we have to inquire into its continuing powers to maintain and restore unity, powers which depend on the hold which the common goal has on the Communists' minds. As the Party confronts challenges, dissension, or other threats to its power and "mission," it is likely to summon up reserves of ideological commitment in order to reinforce unity, increase its momentum, and replenish its purposeful energy. Even at first glance it does not appear probable that an idea-oriented organization would be subject to a steady erosion of its sources of energy which it could do nothing to stem. Rather, one would expect that in periodic crises the Party would go through renewals of its original commitment. The Party is based on the assumption of irreconcilable hostility against a deadly enemy, and the fear of a "restoration" has played no small part in its history. Both this fear and this hate would be renewed, and ideological orthodoxy in some form restored, whenever internal or external enemies seemed to threaten the Party. The disposition to "split," i.e. separate itself from incompatible company, will likely come to the fore from time to time. Thus Communist evolution probably will occur less along the line of a steady process of decline than in waves of ideological intensification, followed by periods of coasting, until another basic challenge confronts the Party. This general surmise is, by and large, borne out by events. The Party's history does not follow a single trend but rather a number of developments that continue for a while and then are brought to an abrupt end, as the Party's leadership decides to tighten discipline and renew revolutionary energies. Among many other examples one may cite the recent renewal of the Party's control of literary production, as well as the Party's intensified persecution of organized religion.

Much speculation concerns the weakening of the Communists' hope in their ultimate goal. In general one must, of course, assume that those who have unrealistic expectations are doomed to bitter disillusionment. In the case of the futuristic ideologies, however, one should use this assumption with reserve. Joachim of Flora, for instance, at the end of the twelfth century, published speculations that the third and final age of history would begin in 1260. When that year came without the promised metamorphosis of the world, the Joachite movement did not die from disappointment but rather continued to push ahead the date of its prophecy. Communism deliberately built into its own ideological structure safeguards against historical disappointment. First, it used the example of the French Revolution for a warning against the pitfalls one must avoid. Secondly, the time for the ultimate fulfillment has never been fixed but rather defined in terms of conditions that must first be attained; thirdly, the designation "protracted struggle" pertains to an indefinite period after the seizure of power, during which period remnants of "bourgeois consciousness" and "anti-Party machinations" are conceded the power to delay history. During all this time, the Party expects to be in the minority, so that reverses are to be expected. The Communists have trained themselves not to be in a hurry. The temptations of the long period of struggle have been enumerated in the ideological scriptures, their knowledge is part of the Party's moral armor.

Actually, however, the history of the last half century can well be summed up by Communists as a series of encouragements rather than disappointments. During the first thirty years, the Communists won no more than Russia. In the twenty years thereafter, though, they obtained control of the whole of Eastern Europe, China, half of Korea, half of Vietnam, and half of Laos. In the last ten years they have gained an important bridgehead in Latin America that now seems to enjoy the guarantee of the U.S.A., the only power capable of eliminating it. In addition, they have won important allies in the Middle East and Africa. At any rate, a Communist need not look at this half century as a refutation of the prophecy underlying the doctrine of the protracted struggle.

What about the continued refusal of human reality to mold itself to the pattern Communist ideology postulates? Whenever the world does not behave in accordance with the ideology, the ideologist can either correct his views or else seek to correct the world. In so far as he corrects his views, one must watch closely which elements of the ideology he is willing to abandon and for what ideas. One can characterize Communists as those Marxists who in repeated crises have been willing to give up parts of the ideology provided the doctrine of the revolutionary overthrow of the present-day society was not touched. In a moment of sober review of Marxism, at the end of the nineteenth century, Eduard Bernstein concluded that the doctrine of the revolution had been refuted by history and that the class struggle should henceforth be understood as an effort to reform society and lift social morality. Faced with the same historical evidence, Lenin clung above all to the revolutionary dogma and was willing to modify other parts of Marx's ideology instead. His option then has since constituted the hallmark of Communist thinking. Later choices of Communist leadership have followed the pattern set by Lenin. This is true even of those major decisions which may look to us like retreats, compromises, or departures from the core of the ideology. The NEP looked to most people like a sacrifice of essential Marxist principles, but it turned out to be merely a form of *reculer pour mieux sauter* (a few steps back in order to gain momentum for the main leap forward). The next crisis confronted the Communists between 1924 and 1927 when the question of how to obtain for the regime the produce of the countryside arose with great urgency. Bukharin was then in favor of scrapping that part of the ideology which called for the "vanquishing" of the peasantry and its way of life; Trotsky demanded that the peasantry be subjected by means of forceful controls. Bukharin's advice in a sense resembled that of Bernstein, in that it envisaged calling off the class struggle as a concept of existential hostility. Stalin, having first sided with Bukharin to eliminate Trotsky from the Party, then adopted Trotsky's course. A similar choice was necessary later on between an investment policy that would have favored consumer industries and one that placed priority on heavy industry, the basis of power. Malenkov is reported to have favored the first course after 1950. Khrushchev, having first beaten Malenkov out of the Party's leading position, opted for priority on heavy industry. The pattern so far is consistent: when in doubt the Party leadership has always chosen that alternative which favored irreconcilable struggle and its power requirements. The past, however, has no power to bind, and it is always possible that the Communist leadership one day will take the path that Bernstein and Bukharin advocated. Hitherto, though, those Marxists or Communists who desired to modify the will to struggle and unmitigated class hostility have usually dropped out of the ranks of Party leaders and ended up with the stamp of deviation or treason on them.

While the past does not eliminate the basic freedom of human wills, in the case of the Communists it is part of the official indoctrination. Party history is taught as a source of ideology, and past options have been surrounded by dogma. A decision to advocate a Bernstein-Bukharin alternative when faced with external difficulties would therefore have to overcome considerable emotional resistance and should not be expected as a matter of course. In order to avoid misunderstandings on this point, mention should be made of the three times in its history when the Party decided to call off a war that had not led to rapid success: Poland, in 1920, Finland, in 1940, and Korea, in 1951. The evaluation of these precedents, however, should not be based on the mistaken assumption that war and naked force have at any time played a key role in Communist ideology, in the way that they did in the Nazi world. From the outset, the Communist ideology has looked on war only as a sociological and political event that would afford the Party opportunities to advance its interests and weaken its enemy.

Loss of Élan?

In so far as one can speak of an evolutionary pattern of the Communist movement, one can hardly maintain that it has consisted of a steady decline of "revolutionary zeal" and a steadily increasing interest in nonideological views and activities. Naturally, a party in control of a country has different problems and concerns from those of a party seeking to loosen up a country's social fabric. In Russia, the Communists have even done much to strengthen a somewhat Victorian morality, not because they abandoned their Communist views on bourgeois morality but because this moral severity was useful to minimize unnecessary trouble among their subjects. The ideological core, however, the will to fight to the death against "imperialism" and "the monopolists," has not gradually weakened but rather risen to several crests in the course of time, each time accompanied by renewals of deep concern with the dangers allegedly threatening the Party. Other fighting movements in history have likewise demonstrated a power to rise to wave upon wave of recrudescence. Islam is a case in point, with the last religious wave, the movement of the Wahabites, coming early in our century, and Nasser's Arab nationalism constituting a secularized new version. Communism is much younger than Islam, which, of course, does not commit one to the conclusion that it must continue the same amount of time as Islam. All the same, its short history contains no evidence justifying the assumption of a trend toward "liberalism." On the contrary, those among Communists who may have come to doubt the future of a classless society, or the world-historical mission of the Party, or the total unworthiness of capitalism, have quit being Communists, either voluntarily or involuntarily. At any rate, even should they remain in the Party, such men are unlikely to rise very high. Those who speak of a mutation of "Communism" fail to show what reason Communists could have to preserve discipline and unity if it were not for the common hope and the common struggle in which they believe. When the ideological cement crumbles the Party will not long stay in one piece. Some of its factions might continue to operate for a while, in a panic quest for survival, but they would do so without a sense of direction, confidence, or hope. One cannot doubt that this end will come one day. At the same time, nobody should permit his ardent desire for that day to create illusions that bar his perception of present realities.

CHAPTER 5

How to Fail in Government
Without Really Trying

One of the perennial arguments denying the ideological character of Communism points to the Communists' success, which it claims would not have been possible if the Communists really had followed their own ideology. The argument relies on demonstrably false assumptions about Communist successes. First, judged on its own ideological pretensions, Communism must be called a total failure. Secondly, in so far as it has achieved constructive objectives, they have been made possible only at the price of serious imbalances in the whole of society. Thirdly, certain policies have created what one must call a condition of chronic failure. Fourthly, other policies have been persistently pursued even though they corresponded to no practical need and constituted sheer ideological self-indulgence.

No Renewal of Life

According to the Communist ideology, the development of the "new society" after the overthrow of capitalism proceeds in two phases, of which the lower one is called "socialism" and the higher one "Communism." In 1936 Stalin proclaimed the "lower stage" completed, and in 1955 Molotov was resoundingly rapped on the knuckles when, in a slip of the tongue, he spoke of the construction of "socialism" as a still ongoing process. Though this lower stage supposedly is "still afflicted with the birthmarks of the old society," it would presumably be free from exploitation. Marx attributed the exploitative evils of capitalism to two economic conditions which he called "commodity production" and the "law of value" (*Capital*, Vol. I). Both were supposed to disappear along with the abolition of private ownership of the means of production. In 1953, however, Stalin himself declared that "commodity production" and the "law of value" still obtained in the Soviet Union and would continue there for an indefinite period (*Economic Problems of Socialism in the USSR*, 1953). Nor has exploitation disappeared. The Soviets periodically boast of the rising productivity of their workers, but wages have been kept at an average level of $70–$80 a month; no collective bargaining is permitted; unions are "company"-oriented agencies whose main objective is to get top performances out of the workers; work is determined by norms set by shock brigades and is largely remunerated on a piece basis. Regarding the promise that the "free development of each" would be the "condition for the free development of all," the only persons to enjoy freedom in the Soviet Union are the leading members of the Communist Party. According to the ideology, crime would wane as soon as capitalism had disappeared. In the Soviet Union, not only does conventional crime persist, but new types of crime have sprung up and resulted in entire groups living outside of the law on the margin of society. After half a century of Communist rule, there is no sign of a new culture. On the contrary, when Russians even today think of "culture," they can envisage it only in the forms which it had in 1914, which forms they still use to build houses, decorate rooms—even to design modern airplanes, paint art, and compose music. A socialist revolution was supposed to be an event liberating men from all kinds of social inequities and limitations. Judging by the original conception, no socialist revolution was ever consummated, in Russia or elsewhere.

The Albatross of the Peasant Problem

Agriculture is the area of Communist policy that can be called a chronic failure, because the policy has been determined ideologically to the point of economic self-immolation. When Lenin, in 1905, decided on a Communist takeover "in alliance" with the peasantry, he also called the peasantry "unreliable" and "vacillating" and decreed a future campaign of the Party against its erstwhile allies. In 1928 Stalin spoke of the peasantry as "classes hostile to us" and asserted that mere state planning could not overcome their resistance. What then happened can only be called a case of violent aggression by a regime against the major part of its subjects, perpetrated at a cost of six to eight million lives, conservatively estimated. Russian agriculture has never recovered from the blow of collectivization. Its productivity has remained far below that of other industrialized or industrializing countries. To this day, more than 40 percent of the population are required for agricultural work, each Russian farmer producing only enough for himself and one urban dweller, while no more than 5 percent of the U.S. population work on farms and produce a surplus that sustains millions in foreign countries.

To this failure the Communist Party has reacted quixotically. Periodically, private plots and private livestock in narrow limits have been granted to the farmers and then taken away again, only to be restored later. In the early Fifties, the Party envisaged the creation of agro-towns, city-like settlements of farmers whence they would be driven to work as far as fifty miles every morning. Later, collective farms were consolidated in order to increase the leverage of bureaucratic control. Then Khrushchev launched his disastrous "virgin land" enterprise, bureaucratically shifting a large population to hitherto uninhabited areas. A concession like the turning over of farm machinery from separate machine and tractor stations to the collective farms was offset by manipulation of agricultural prices through the state farms. All this is a textbook example of what Marx calls "despotic inroads . . . measures, therefore, which appear economically insufficient and untenable . . . but which, in the course of the movement, outstrip themselves, necessitate further inroads . . ." Do Communists look upon collectivization of agriculture as a miscalculation which they now regret? The Chinese Communists, fully aware of the failure in Soviet agriculture, launched on the same course as late as 1956, with even higher speed and more radical objectives. True, in Yugoslavia and Poland collectivization was abandoned, but at the same time, in East Germany and Hungary it was pressed forward. Nobody can rightly claim that the Communist agricultural policy was either a political or an economic necessity, for Poland has proved that agricultural production can be increased under a Communist regime by returning it to private initiative, and even in Russia the economic success of the farmers' private plots has been spectacular. Collectivized agriculture, on the other hand, has become the bottleneck that obstructs the growth of the entire Soviet economic system.

For an example of a policy that netted the Communists no gains but many difficulties, one should take the persecution of religion. By 1926 the leaders of the Russian Orthodox Church had declared their willingness to abide by the regime. At that time the Communists decided on a frontal assault on the Church, replete with imprisonments and executions, the closing of churches, monasteries, and seminaries, and the harassment of the faithful. When in 1941 all resources of allegiance were needed to see the regime through the war, a truce with the Church became official policy. After the war, however, Communists renewed the attack with changed methods, infiltrating the clergy, splitting the Church from the inside, playing off one part against another. In the Sixties, the official persecution of clergy and believers was once more intensified, while a few open churches were dressed up as showplaces to placate world opinion. In a profoundly Christian country, a policy of coexistence with the Church chould have netted the Communists considerable political capital. Poland is a clear case of political weakness that comes to a Communist regime from opposing the Church. All the same, anti-Church policies have not abated; only methods have been changed from time to time. In Hungary and Czechoslovakia the Roman Catholic Church organization has been reduced to near ruins. It is obvious that Communist policy here springs from no pursuit of political power *per se* but from ideological commitment to antitheism.

Economic Mismanagement

Similar irrationalities have beset Communist economic policies, particularly prices, wages, and marketing. Wages have been used largely as a means to achieve political objectives. Prices have been fixed in accordance with the labor theory of value which no self-respecting economist today will consider except for historical purposes. The resulting maladjustments in Soviet internal accounting have been officially noted by commission after commission endeavoring to introduce some order into Soviet bookkeeping. Soviet helplessness in this respect is illustrated by the incapacity of the Soviet authorities to determine the value of a commodity without referring to world market prices. The Soviet method of price-fixing has distorted the ruble as a yardstick for the comparison of values. Throughout the Soviet economy the ruble has varied, from as much as 80 cents for agricultural commodities delivered to the state down to 1 or 2 cents on consumer goods. The Communists have treated the economy not so much as the basis for a people's material wellbeing, as for the purposes of power, particularly armaments and heavy industry. They have given disproportional preference to spectacular achievements that had both military and propaganda value; for instance, space rocketry, and in selected areas have so concentrated their energies that they have on occasion outproduced Western countries. In order to do this, however, they neglected, until as late as the Sixties, to develop even a chemical industry, thereby further aggravating their agricultural plight. Vast areas of the Soviet economy lack machinery required for modern production while others are as sophisticated as tomorrow. In view of such failures, Communist policies from time to time have sought to shift the burden to other shoulders. From the early Thirties, for a period of twenty years, millions of political prisoners were pressed into slave labor. After the war, POWs replaced them, while reparations supplemented the Soviet shortages. Labor camps have now given way to "forced residence." All along, the burden of Soviet investment has been harshly imposed on the peasantry. For more than a decade after the war, the Russian Communists also exploited their satellites, using them to pay for Soviet economic irrationalities. Lately, they have returned to an old and tried source of aid in need: the West. Since the introduction of the "peaceful-coexistence" policy, the West has increasingly furnished the Soviets with machines, food, technology, ever widening trade on long-term credit. Entire factories which the Soviets did not build because of their distorted priorities, sophisticated electronic machines for which they would not assign skilled manpower, food to make up for the defects of a mismanaged agriculture have gone to postpone the day of reality's reckoning with the Communist regime.

The yardstick that permits us to call Communist economic management irrational is, of course, a moral one that sees an economic system not only as the provider for material needs but also as a system compatible with individual freedom. That the Communist system has not delivered either of these goods is notorious. One must not forget, though, that from the point of view of an aggressive militant enterprise, it has indeed served its purpose. The Party has drawn from the economy of Russia offensive and defensive armaments second only to those of the United States, funds for a propaganda machinery that has no equal and, indeed, no precedent, and the means for worldwide programs of power expansion which no possible conception of Russia's security could justify. In terms of ideological struggle, Communist economic management has not done badly at all.

So *this* much for Communist reactions to reality. How about Communist reactions to favorable developments? This relation is difficult to capture in an equation, for one lacks the measure of what a normal government would have done under the circumstances. The difference may become discernible when Communists present to the world radical and excessive demands which nevertheless are conceded, so that one would have to call the Communists satisfied on their own showing, except that they turn out to be as dissatisfied as before. Hitler provides suitable precedents. The *Anschluss* of Austria had been a maximal but unattainable foreign policy objective of both Germans and Austrians. Hitler obtained it in 1938. Then came the series of negotiations, or rather, succession of ultimatums with ever increased antes that led to Munich, where England and France gave Hitler everything which even the wildest German patriotism could dream of, so that by all standards of normal politics Germany should have been a sated power. It turned out that Hitler's concrete demands did not represent his limitless will to power but rather only his concept of strategy. He immediately turned on Czechoslovakia, and, within a year, on Poland. By the end of 1940 Hitler was master of Europe to a far greater extent than Napoleon had ever been, and his position was protected by Russia's consent and not seriously threatened by Britain. What had been realized was no longer a merely patriotic aspiration but the dream of a conqueror of European stature. Again, this compliance of reality failed to satisfy Hitler. He attacked Russia and, in December 1941, even took the initiative in declaring war on the United States.

Foreign Policy Without Limits

Communist foreign policy followed a similar pattern. The defeat of Germany and Japan had secured Russia's existence in East and West as it had never been secured before. The smaller East European countries had voluntarily adopted an obligation to abide by a Russophile policy and a conciliatory attitude toward their own domestic Communists. All this would have more than satisfied Peter the Great and Catherine. The Communists, however, moved on from there. They violated their solemn pledge and installed Party-controlled regimes in the entire satellite belt. When the Soviet Union in 1949 also obtained a nuclear capability she could esteem herself as safe from any outside attack as any country would wish to be. Precisely this moment, however, was the beginning of new ventures. Korea, in which the U. S. A. had publicly declared herself disinterested, was invaded. Two years after this conflict had ended in a draw, President Eisenhower at Geneva gave the Communist leaders every possible assurance of peaceful intention. The next year, Communist arms sales to the Middle East stirred up trouble there, then came a new ultimatum on Berlin, and by the end of the Fifties the Communists began operations in Southeast Asia, Africa, and Latin America, finally moving into Cuba with heavy offensive weaponry. Like Hitler, the Communists seem to be people incapable of satisfaction by concrete attainments. From what must be judged secure and advantageous positions they have again and again moved outward into ventures that could only arouse new forces of resistance again them. What the Soviets consider threats to their security—American rearmament, NATO, and the Western alliance system, the ring of U. S. bases around the USSR—have been brought on by the Communists' refusal to leave well enough alone. The concept of a status quo seems to be alien to the Communist mind. Whatever appears to the Communists as a settlement, a concretely defined proposal of mutual concession and satiation, also is suspect in their eyes as counterrevolutionary, a betrayal of that basic discontent that will never come to rest in present-day society. If Walter Lippmann has correctly reported the interview which he had with Khrushchev in November 1958, the Communist commitment to insatiability came out clearly then: "In his mind," wrote Lippmann, "the social and economic revolution now in progress in Russia, China and elsewhere in Asia and Africa *is* the status quo, and he wants us to recognize it as such. In his mind, opposition is an attempt to change the status quo. Whereas we think of the status quo as the situation as it exists at the moment, he thinks of it as the process of revolutionary change which is in progress. He wants us to recognize the revolution not only as it is but as it is going to be." (*The Communist World and Ours*, 1958) To recognize not what is but what "is becoming"— that is to see "dialectically"!

De-Stalinization

As a last example of Communist conflict with reality let us consider de-Stalinization. One might say that in the spring of 1953 the entire Communist regime had been rent by its inner contradictions, to the point of collapse. The practice of perennial purge through which the Party expected to "grow stronger," the practically unlimited power of the secret police, functioning like an occupying military power, the concentration of all power in an individual's hands had produced such widespread personal insecurity that Party discipline was jeopardized. Government by Communists along Stalin's lines was no longer possible. The reality which the Communists had to face was not that of outside forces: it was their own failure to create a viable political order. At the moment of Stalin's death, something like political bankruptcy stared the surviving Party leaders in the face. It was their own manner of ruling that had come to the end of its tether.

In true Communist style, de-Stalinization was a strategic retreat but not a change of heart or a return to sanity. The blame was laid on the dead despot but the survivors and, indeed, the system as a whole were exonerated. Khrushchev's famous denunciatory speech of February 25, 1956, blamed the latter part of Stalin's life but left beyond criticism the earlier period in which Stalin had led the Party to collectivization of the countryside, set up the police state, banished and assassinated Trotsky, dogmatized the ideology, and subjected labor to a harshly regimented exploitation. In other words, it was essentially the personal temperament of an aging autocrat that was indicted. Stalin's name, statues, and books disappeared, but his foundations and even his teachings remained part and parcel of the official system.

The use of Stalin's personality as a lightning rod, however, is not the heart of de-Stalinization. For that one must look at the alleged "reforms" embodied in the Party Program of 1961. We can classify these alleged concessions under three headings: a) the assertion that the dictatorship of the proletariat had come to an end; b) the assertion that its place had been taken by a new state concept called "socialist democracy" or "state of the whole people"; c) the assertion that the "withering away of the state" had already begun with the devolution of state functions onto "social organizations." These concessions, at first glance, impress us as small but real steps toward democratization. As one looks closer, however, one finds that the substance of Party dictatorship has been maintained although the methods have been changed from overt to covert ones. The substance of Party dictatorship can be said to consist of four features: The Communist Party's monopoly of power, its use of governmental machinery for its own strategic purposes, subordination of the judiciary to the Party's conflict purposes, and systematic official use of terror. In short, the political order has been made a tool of the Party's goals, and the attribute "proletarian" has had no meaning at all. The new Party Program was accompanied by a number of changes in practice. The powers of the Secret Police were curtailed, the barbed wire removed from labor camps, executions went out of fashion, the overt forms of terror were sharply reduced. If, however, one measures dictatorship in terms of the above-mentioned four characteristics, one finds that the Party still holds the monopoly not only of political power but of social organization in general; the entire governmental and social structure still serves as a means to realize the Party's purposes; the law is still operated as a tool of the "class struggle"; terror is still ubiquitous, in the more covert but no less effective forms of social intimidation, isolation of individuals, and Party-directed organization of fear. The authorities still spy on their fellow citizens and refuse to tolerate the slightest show of opposition, even though they may take their time about doing so. The new state concept does not commit the Party to share its power or to permit other than Communist ideas, to give room to people's spontaneity, to acknowledge the majesty of an objective law, or to give up the weapon of terror.

Under the name "socialist democracy" the new program introduced certain institutional "reforms," namely: a three-term limit of eligibility to public office, a reduction of salaried staffs in favor of part-time employees, punishment of bureaucrats for "abuse of power," and a modicum of public influence as a substitute for governmental authority. The most important of these is the periodic renewal of the leading governmental bodies. This principle might indeed constitute the beginning of genuine democracy if it applied to the top group of leaders in the Kremlin. If, however, it applied only to the lower echelons while those on top remained in place, it would strengthen the Party's hold on the bureaucratic machinery and institutionalize a perpetual and bloodless purge. Blaming the bureaucracy for the failings of the Party's regime is traditional in the Soviet Union. What is more, the bureaucracy has possessed the only effective power of resistance to the Party within the system. One can see all of Khrushchev's reforms as having a double meaning: an appearance of democratization and a reality of increased Party domination. Nonsalaried, part-time employees are easier to manipulate than professionals. Punishment for "abuse of power" is both popular with the masses and useful in dealing with obstreperous officials. The substitution of "public influence" for governmental action serves the same end, since no "public influence" is allowed to take shape without Party direction and control. Finally, the "withering away" of the state turns out to be nothing more than the turning over of state functions to nongovernmental bureaucratic machineries which are fully controlled by the Party: the trade unions and the Komsomols (the Party's youth organization). In Lenin's book, the "withering away of the state" was supposed to consist in the disappearance of state functions as such, but the new Program retains these functions and simply confers them on other tools of the Party's will. Both the trade unions and the Komsomols have effective power to grant or deny to people the necessities of life and thus impose painful penalties for nonconformity. The Party, in other words, has dispersed and disguised its controls in an effort to conceal them from the people and from world opinion.

When Communists find themselves clashing with human, social, economic, or political realities they either try to burden others with the cost of this conflict or else seek increased power to bend reality to their preconceived image. They may also shift their methods or beat a temporary retreat. One reaction alone is not found in the Communist record: They do not allow reality to correct their basic ideas. If reality differs from their ideas it is reality that is wrong, not their thinking. A generation may come that finds itself at a loss for further evasions, or excuses, or shifting maneuvers. There are certain signs, though, by which one could tell that this had occurred, and in a later chapter we shall turn to that question.

CHAPTER 6

Rationality

in Communist Practice

Two Kinds of Rationality

One should distinguish between substantive and pragmatic rationality, the former a rationality of outlook and interpretation of reality, the latter a rational choice of means to given ends of whatever kind. Communism amounts to a profoundly irrational view of man, society, history, and political purposes, the substitution of a dream world for reality, and the denial of a common human condition. That, however, is only one aspect of Communism. The other is a doctrine of operation that was developed by Lenin in answer to his own central question, "What is to be done?" meaning "What is to be done about the basic Communist view of man, society, and history?" These basic views are to a Communist, dogmas never to be questioned or even examined. Communists thus do all their thinking only within the pragmatic area which they define as the "period of transition" and characterize as a "protracted struggle." Whether it makes sense to view the area of pragmatic action as a "period of transition," implying that one already knows where this transition will lead, is not for them to ask. These basic premises being settled, Communists concentrate entirely on the relation between the Party and the masses, the strategic assessment of forces hostile and friendly, the fine distinctions between thought and actions deemed "'revolutionary" and those called "reactionary." If it were true that the Communists' protracted struggle was indeed history's road to man's ultimate fulfillment of his destiny, then one would have to call Communist strategic thinking a masterfully logical method of means and ways to attain the end. One may call this thinking pragmatic rationality, provided one remembers that the "perfect crime" is also a type of pragmatic rationality.

The distinction should serve to cure us from the silly notion that Communists, or others who act on deeply irrational premises, must look and act like wild men. Communists in particular are sober, unemotional, almost pedantic in their language, not easily provoked, methodical. Communists above all are used to dealing with power, their own and their enemy's, and trained to refrain from battle when the odds are against them. The kind of strategic madness that made Hitler bid German armies to stay and bleed to death in hopeless positions is quite alien to the Communist mind. What is more, even a certain amount of constructive rationality has room within the basic irrational purpose that is characteristic of Communism. A tyrant, even though he may inhabit an ideological dream world, can go about building his power by organizing resources, mobilizing manpower, and manipulating skills so as to produce missiles, spaceships, and nuclear bombs. All this can create the illusion of genuine rationality in a web of seemingly sober actions. But then the man who fancies himself the Emperor of China can also be said to behave rationally, if one accepts the single premise of his conduct. Thus a purely instrumental rationality should not be allowed to obscure the substantive irrationality embodied in a basic refusal to accept the human condition. Above all, however, from the irrational premises of Communism will come courses of action which in no wise fit into a rational framework and which we, the people outside, cannot logically predict. That is why Churchill rightly called the Soviets a mystery in a riddle wrapped in an enigma: even when they appear to be at their most rational, the unpredicted and unpredictable may ensue at any time without warning.

Limitless Goals, Limited Stratagems

It is these moments of unaccountable conduct that have nourished the Western caricature of the Communist's looking or acting like a madman or criminal. The reason is that we incline to attribute to Communists the basic views about man and society that we hold, and then blame their "excesses" on temperament, upbringing, indignation, frustration, or some other psychological cause. What is so very difficult for Westerners to grasp is the premise which Lenin drove deep into the Communist mind, that total destruction of our society is the price demanded by history for progress. Even though we may accept the idea that Communists consider themselves locked with us in mortal struggle, we still incline to think of it as a kind of grand military engagement, with forces lined up on both sides for a showdown of force. Lenin, however, took no such cheap view of the Revolution's business. The job to which he committed his movement is one of revolutionary destruction, not merely of national power but of the entire fabric of society. He took great pains to make all Communists realize that this fabric is complex, extremely hard and durable, and always capable of producing power for action. The keynote of Leninism is the rejection of the single battle or frontal assault concept. Lenin almost ridiculed the notion that driving out the capitalists and landowners and abolishing private property could really break the old social order. It had strength to survive, he said, in countless institutions, relations, and above all in the "terrible force of habit." Hence Lenin adopted a condition for the struggle which one might call "irreconcilable normality." The destruction of the enemy is to be viewed as a long-term proposition, and meanwhile one must coexist with him. One has to share his institutions, gestures, even his aspirations, but all the while remain intent on "vanquishing" him. The Communists, in a sense, recognize a relationship of common rationality, but they intend never to live within it except for the purpose of totally subverting it.

It would be a mistake to see this condition in terms of small trickery. When the Communists speak of coexistence they are sincere in the sense that that is a relationship they have decided to accept. To be more specific, if the Communist Party of a country declares that it wants to run its own candidates for parliamentary election, one should not assume that their sole purpose is to get into the building in order to blow it up. On the other hand, however, one must understand the two reservations Communists always have in mind regarding any coexistence: first, they cannot possibly accept with any sense of obligation any of the institutions or authorities that pertain to the present-day society. In their eyes, the present-day society is totally condemned and totally doomed, and no decent man could consider himself bound to it in loyalty. The evil of class rule has penetrated its tissue to the core. Moreover, the Communists are convinced that it is a has-been society and would feel utterly foolish if it might occur to them to look upon it as a place in which to settle. The second reservation is contained in the principle of flexibility of all methods, which is at the heart of Leninism. Thus coexistence can be seen as a form of struggle which does not even preclude the use of overt force here and there. The writings and authoritative speeches of Communists again and again exhort the Party to be ready for abrupt switches of methods, which may mean from overt clash of force to peaceful coexistence, but also the reverse. At one and the same time Communists may even pursue two mutually exclusive policies, as they did, for instance, in France and Spain where they both supported and sought to destroy their coalition partners, and as they do in some Latin American countries where they both endorse and secretly fight an established dictatorship.

Given the Communist premise, that the present-day society is wholly and hopelessly inhuman, such strategies are neither illogical nor irrational. What *is* irrational is the basic assumption, the combination of a total condemnation of the present with the certainty that something wholly different and utterly good will emerge in the future. This is what makes Communists persuade themselves that they are working for the love of humanity when they seek to break traditional loyalties, habits, thoughts, and beliefs and to put individual men, spiritually and morally denuded, under the totalitarian direction of the Party. One must firmly believe in a "Second Reality" to regard this as a rational purpose. Once one does, however, one must concede that the Communists have developed remarkable skill in gauging human strengths and weaknesses, mixing pressure with persuasion, isolating their victims and even obtaining their consent to their own undoing. They deserve scientific awards for their methods of breaking moral backbones and eroding inner resistances through mixtures of emotion and reason. We are quite well informed about the procedure which one writer unfortunately has called "brainwashing." The term is unfortunate because it conjures up the notion of man as a being who can be chemically manipulated at will. The Communists themselves, however, know better, as is proved by their method, for which a more adequate designation is *Communist Persuasions*, the title of a remarkable book by Eleutherius Winance (New York, 1958). Winance describes the process as an oscillation between fear-begetting pressure and fear-releasing reasoning, a description which parallels that given by Czeslav Milosz in his *The Captive Mind* (1951). Understood as these writers understand it, the Communist treatment of individual enemies can serve as a key to the understanding of their strategies at large. If Westerners continue to be puzzled by Communist policies, it is because they fail to use the proper keys: number one, the irrational purpose dictating the total destruction of the present-day society as the requisite for a total future goodness, and two, the pragmatic thoroughness with which Communists go about implementing this purpose in analysis and action. In the words of Melville's Captain Ahab: "All my means are sane: my motives and object mad."

Communist Realism

Another way of stating the paradox of Communist rationality in the execution of Communist irrationality is to point out that while basic Communist thinking moves not in reality but in a dream world, Communist practice takes shape in a very sober appreciation of reality that is remarkably free from ideological distortion. This, however, applies only to the analysis, planning, and methods of struggle, in which realm Communists consider realism as the highest revolutionary virtue. Again, the underlying irrational premise teaches that society and life are nothing but an irreconcilable struggle between adamantly hostile forces, so that to struggle *à outrance* appears as a dictate of sobriety. Once in the struggle, however, Communists want to look at things as they are. At that point, they pay little attention to the historical materialism that defines the human mind as determined by the economic foundations of society. On the contrary, the Communists postulate that what holds the Party together is consciousness, that the greatest and strongest resisting power of the bourgeoisie is the residual bourgeois consciousness, and that what brings about a revolutionary situation is a certain state of mind in both the ruling and the ruled classes. In other words, when it comes to the laws of struggle, the Communists recognize the human mind as the focus of their efforts, and are unwilling to consider their work done when they have removed or abolished economic institutions. In this respect, the Communists move on solid grounds of experience. For the ultimate *locus* of political reality is in men's minds. The Communists' single-minded concentration on the human mind is hardly in keeping with historical materialism, but precisely for that reason has met with considerable success. For the same reason, Communist strategy never relies chiefly or exclusively on force. They would think very poorly of a victory that left an enemy's army in defeat but his society intact. What Communists seek is leverage to subvert the entire social, political, and moral order, through control of people's minds.

The pragmatic rationality of Communists appears incomprehensible only when one overlooks the irrational premise on which it operates. At present, much of the Communist struggle is conducted in the field of international relations, or "politics among nations," as Morgenthau has called it. The rational dimension of international politics is what is commonly called power politics, i.e. relations with a view to national security or national rank in terms of power relative to the power of other nations. There are many who call power politics irrational, because it is politics conducted not under the auspices of, or with a view to, government but in a governmentless web of relations between armed units. True, the rationality of a common political order is absent from international relations. All the same, the limitation of rivalry and reciprocal concern to the power problem is a rationality of sorts, for it leaves untouched the various societies as such, the various orders through which and in which men live ordered lives in company with like-minded fellow beings and in possession of cherished traditions. International politics concerns only power, i.e. only an external aspect of society, the amount of influence a government has in relation to other governments. Even wars are waged mainly with a view to power and cease when the chief instruments of power, the armed forces, have been contested and some kind of certainty about their relative strength has been established.

In this sense, the Communist thrust aims not merely at power. Power is but a stage on the way to the realization of its purpose which embraces the social order as such. Power is an eminently political reality beyond which there lie other dimensions of human existence. The Communist struggle uses the political to penetrate these other dimensions. In its ultimate conception, the Communist struggle should not be called political, and the appearance of a great Communist power on the world scene has done much to destroy the political character of international relations. What this Communist power seeks is more than an increment in power. When it obtains a victory, the result will affect more than the external aspects of a society; it will penetrate to the core of the social order and seek to change it from its natural existence into something else. In his novel, *The Cancer Ward*, Aleksandr Solzhenitzyn made this same point through the analogy of the doctors' treatment of a patient's malignant tumor. The prescription, in this case, was for hormone injections that would deprive a man of his virility and a woman of her femininity. The hero of the story refused to submit to this kind of treatment, particularly since no doctor was as yet certain that the treatment would assuredly lead to success, but above all because the treatment would destroy his essence as a male human being. Medical treatment going beyond the limits of therapy and embracing the core of human nature, in Solzhenitzyn's novel, is the analog to international relations going beyond the limit of a struggle for power and embracing the core of social existence.

Given the Communist brushing aside of the rational

limitations of international politics, however, the Communist operations in the struggle appear as a logical conclusion.

The power of a society is a secondary phenomenon, resulting from the fact that people who share a common life have something in common that is basic to the existence of all, so that they speak of the whole as "we." Wherever that is the case, the community is potentially capable of producing leadership for action in history, and thereby power. A pure power struggle in the international arena leaves this potency intact, even though it affects the external vector of power. The Communists, however, have concentrated their efforts on the social foundations of power, which are common truths, mutual trust and friendship, legitimate authority, and voluntary obedience to it. They have realized that power consists not in mere possession of certain means, as, e.g., material products, raw materials, money, arms, and armed forces, but also in the will and political capability to use such means. An attack on these foundations of power doubly serves the Communists' ultimate purpose: on the one hand, it paralyzes wholly or partially the degree of military resistance which they are likely to encounter; on the other, it promotes the decomposition of the enemy's society as such and thus readies the scene for organized manipulation by the Communist Party. From the Communist point of view, on open and head-on war would indeed be far less suitable strategy than an extended operation which left the enemy's society less capable of producing power and leadership. In the kind of operation the Communists actually conduct, there is no such thing as a victory that could be marked by a peace treaty, because the objective is the gradual weakening of social bonds, the opening of fissures, the discrediting of leadership and, indeed, of the whole of society, the stifling of mutual trust, and the weakening of the will to exist. War can be used in such operations, but war so used would be an occasion rather than the main instrument of Communist operations. In any case, the main interest Communists have in war is its indirect psychological effects, such as the loosening of the bonds of order it occasionally brings about. In this context, the users or war appear quite different from those of the power struggle that used to be the rationale of international relations.

If one takes a general look at what we call propaganda and what in Communist terminology is agitation, one cannot deny to the Communists a top grade for extraordinary realism. Communists are people who join the Communist Party because of their acceptance of the Communist ideological view of man, society, and history. Even if their endorsement of that ideology is lukewarm or hesitant at the beginning, Party membership is a process in which their entire personality will be made over in the image of the "Bolshevik," the serious, reliable, versatile, no-nonsense revolutionary. Ideas play a central role in the mentality and the orientation of Communists. Yet the Communist effort at influencing other people relies astonishingly little on direct persuasion in Communist ideology. This fact may not be so astonishing when one remembers that Communists look on themselves as a small band of elect, the exclusive possessors of the truth of history which is not suitable for the masses living from day to day in the present. It is their knowledge, their *gnosis,* which existentially separates the Communists from the rest of mankind, the ordinary human beings living in past and present, while the Communists make their abode in the future. This division of all men into two levels with no common floor causes the Communists to entrust the arcana only to those who are fit to become active Party members.

All other people are approached, not in terms of the Communist ideology, but of their own natural or political concerns or aspirations. To be sure, the Communists want them on their side, but only in a position which they call "support for the Party." They bid for support by appearing to identify themselves with such strong, simple, widespread desires or aversions as "peace," "national independence," "democracy," "antifascism," "disarmament." None of these represents directly the Communist ideology and its view of either present or future. By Lenin's strict admonition, Communists are not pacifists but are willing to use violence on a small or a large scale, to unleash or incite wars, to go to war, and in general to fight with the hardest determination. Nor are Communists in favor of national independence, a fact that, if it were not attested by the ideological scriptures, could be easily gleaned from the occupation of Czechoslovakia and the Brezhnev Doctrine of "limited sovereignty." Democracy for Communists is only a means to the end of their victory, and so are the remaining notions. All the same, it is through their public identification with such desires or aversions that they obtain large-scale influence over people who in no wise are convinced of Communist ideology. This means that Communist regimes must pursue policies which in themselves do not point to the maximum goal of the socialist Revolution but rather to a minimum program (Lenin's term) by means of which Communists can manipulate broad masses into supporting them. The whole operation is a masterpiece of realism, sprung from Lenin's crystal-clear observation that one must take people as one finds them and where they are. Communist "propaganda," i.e. initiation into Communism's system of ideas, will be reserved for the elect few; agitation is the Communist treatment for all others. It is a widespread misconception, for instance, to expect that a Communist professor in a university will use his position to teach Communism, and to advocate that under the standards of academic freedom he be allowed to do so. A Communist who is a professor will not teach Communism from the lecture platform; rather, he will hide his real conviction and use his office for purposes of political manipulation of unwitting people. He may make some converts to the Party, but this sort of thing is done clandestinely and under cover. His overt activities may simply align him with some groups known as "progressive" or "humane," or create the impression that Communists are reliable, respectable people, or subtly increase the support for Soviet Russian policy objectives.

Besides maneuvering people into positions of support for the Party, Communist agitation aims at weakening or loosening established loyalties. To this end, Comminists seek to make every particular grievance appear as merely an aspect of a general discontent with the whole of society, so that whatever may be wrong at some point is interpreted as proof of an all-pervading general wrong that supposedly can be abolished only with the whole of society. Similarly, they try to reduce all hates to one general hatability, all evils to one single cause, and they seek to identify this cause with the United States. It is typical of this operation that they always argue in terms of a simple polarization, an "either-or" division of forces that leaves no middle ground: "progressives" or "reactionaries," "imperialists" or "exploited," "peace-lovers" or "war-mongers," "fascists" or "antifascists." Hardly any of these pairs of slogans directly represent the Communist ideology, in which one would find rather such concepts as "proletariat," "class struggle," "materialism," "final revolution," "dictatorship of the proletariat," "protracted struggle." These latter belong to the esoteric language, the former to the mode of public appeal. Thus Communists, who have won all their great victories with the help of masses who were not of the Communist persuasion, have learned how to enlist the support of men and women of goodwill whom they cause to believe that any help given to Communist forces will redound to the immediate benefit of mankind.

Communist Flexibility

It is in this area of pragmatic rationality that the Communists, when encountering formidable obstacles, make strategic adjustments which their opponents often call concessions. It was Lenin who, faced with the irresistible German military advance in 1918, and again, with the wholesale breakdown of the Russian economy in 1920, decided that a policy which stubbornly followed principle without regard to circumstances was unworthy of a serious revolutionary and thus built the principle of "compromises" and flexibility right into the Communist ideology. Without Lenin's *Left-Wing Communism* and his articles and pamphlets on the NEP, Communism might have become one of the short-lived radical sects which from lack of practical effectiveness are unable to hold a place on the world scene. The NEP, falsely labeled a "return to capitalism," was not a "concession" to the other side but rather the strategic move which alone enabled the Communist revolution to advance. De-Stalinization, as worked out between 1953 and 1956, whatever its indirect effects may have been, served directly to reestablish the authority of the Party in Russia, where under Stalin it had been greatly diminished. The so-called Liberman reforms succeeded in giving partial solution to a problem which commission after public commission had investigated, deplored, and vainly worked on ever since the early Thirties: the rationality of Soviet price and wage structures. Far from being a concession to capitalism, the reforms provided the Soviets with their first effective method of cost acounting through profits, which, incidentally, neither become the property of the producers nor guarantee them security of position. Nor did the Liberman reforms institute something like a market economy in Russia, an economy in which the priorities of allocation of resources are determined by consumer choices. Even after the Liberman reforms, the amount of resources allocated to consumer industries is decided by the Party, as are the prices of agricultural products, which are governed by the prices charged by state farms.

Other "concessions" come to mind: the Comminists' decision to abandon Austria, which they had no hope of being able to control by themselves, served them as grand bait for their coexistence policy, about which more will be said later. They withdrew from Azerbaijan, called off the Berlin blockade, agreed to a termination of the Korean war, all in recognition of strong resistance which they were not interested in overtly breaking.

This brings up the question of what "interest" it was that

moved them to such concessions. All kinds of theories are offered: the Soviets are mainly interested in the national security of Russia, in world peace, in the relaxation of international tensions, in being accepted by the family of nations, and so on. All of these views identify the concrete objectives of Soviet policy (e.g., Berlin, Greece, Korea, rational management, Party-state relations) with their ultimate goals. If this were true, such decisions of adjustment as we have mentioned would indeed indicate a shift from excessive and abrasive goals to goals which must be deemed reasonable and attainable. In this sense every one of these concessions, beginning with NEP which one prominent Western leader in 1922 greeted with the remark, "Our troubles with Bolshevism are over," stirred unwarranted hopes in the West. Similar reactions ensued when Stalin embraced Russian nationalism, modified his onslaught on the religious organizations, appeared to accept coalition regimes in Eastern Europe, and sat down with Roosevelt and Churchill in what purported to be old-fashioned cooperative conferences on the future of world politics. As often as such hopes were disappointed, they flared up again, undaunted, at Stalin's death, after Khrushchev's secret speech denouncing Stalin, and they could not be doused even by the cold blast of the Soviet invasion of Czechoslovakia.

One look at Lenin's instructions to Communists, however, should dispel this misunderstanding. The "compromises," the "zigs and zags," the pragmatic maneuvers of Communist policy must never be allowed to touch the core of the revolutionary cause. "There are compromises and compromises," Lenin said, when he distinguished between rolling with the punch, refraining from assaulting untakable positions, recognizing the unsuitability of either time or place of an engagement, acknowledging the need to obtain mass control through the loyalties which still prevail among the masses; all this on the one side, and on the other the complete devotion to the destruction of imperialism, the capitalist system, and that kind of total Party power which alone guarantees the advance into the mythical future. He thereby established two dimensions of Communist policy: one, the ideological dimension, as the supreme guide to all Soviet action; the other, the pragmatic dimension, as that field within which flexibility is not only permitted but ideologically required. Pragmatic flexibility occurs in the choice of a multitude of means and methods to the same end and is governed by the Communist resolve to abandon a particular approach as soon as it turns out not to be effective under given circumstances and to pass on to another, or even to employ two different approaches at the same time, which dialectic thinking finds contradictory but not senseless. The NEP was not a change of ultimate views about reality, man, society, history; the Bolshevik goal was never compromised. It never amounted to more than a detour, a temporary retreat to regroup one's forces in order to resume the advance on another front. The same applies to all other "concessions" which the Communists have made.

Thus the concessions of the Soviets do not imply adoption of a nonideological view of reality, abandonment of the ideological goal, a sober acceptance of the human condition as shared by all, and relinquishment of the Party's claim to essential superiority. Nor do the concrete objectives which Soviet policies pursue at any given time represent their ultimate goals. Nor, finally, can anyone outside of the Communist Party draw anything like a logical conclusion from these ultimate goals to the means that in his opinion should be employed to pursue them. The goals, the future, the struggle, the commitment against the present-day society—these are absolutes and the Party's strategies never touch or modify them. The practical objectives, though, which are adopted from time to time on the basis of a pragmatic assessment of forces hostile, friendly, and neutral, of the power of obstacles and of means to overcome them, are the Party's judgment unencumbered by any other imperative than that of strategic efficency, and the Party's judgment is binding on Communist consciences as the sole correct implementation of Communist revolutionary resolve. The Party may conclude alliances with non-Communist or even anti-Communist forces, support or expend this or that Communist Party on the world scene, order revolutionary abrasiveness or a stance of apparent cooperation, advance or retreat, press an engagement or disengage from it, and in all this the Party's judgment is looked upon as the guarantee that the prescribed course does not compromise the revolutionary goal. Thus no concession will in Communist eyes establish something like the order of peace, in which Communists would settle down to live with their fellow beings, having abandoned their will to change everything into the image of their ideology. Whatever the Party may decide, care has been taken to assure that all pragmatic rationality will remain wholly and essentially subordinated to substantive irrationality.

Communists may drive cars, shop for clothes, appear at parties, have love affairs, conduct research, build houses, railroads, and military airplanes, manage businesses and in all this seem rational in the same way that other people are. All these concerns, however, have a different instrumental relation to the Communist orientation toward reality. For what makes a man a Communist is the intellectual acceptance of a Second Reality and his refusal to accept the world of perception and experience as real. There is a willfulness in this substitution of a dream world for the real world, the will to make a system of ideas his world and to subordinate men, things, and relations to it. Hence it is by his sustained will that the Communist lives in basic estrangement, inhabiting not the same world of reality as his fellow beings but, rather, realms of fiction fashioned by ideological dogma. Misconceptions about Communist mentality usually spring from our habit of drawing rash inferences from observed behavior to probable premises, so that we incline to project our own basic premise into those of other people. In an age when one tends to overestimate reason and to assume perfectly rational basic motivations, and thus never even to suspect one's own mind of any trace of irrationality, the grasping of ideological irrationality comes to very few people. Ideological irrationality appears so strange and remote that one wants to disallow its occurrence altogether. This tendency is reinforced by a pervading pragmatism which makes light of all intellectual attempts to grasp the constitution of being, or, for that matter, becoming. It is on this level of the mind, however, that we find ideological irrationality, a demonic if powerful engagement between human consciousness and willful unreality, a resolve to embrace a world that is not. The man who sits next to us at the dinner table may be in the grip of that resolve, and, for all his pleasant small talk, separated from us by a gulf wider than that created by any ordinary criminal intent.

---·•◦◦──◆◇◇◇◆──◦◦•·---

Peaceful Coexistence
and Peaceful Conquest

The Soviets' New Strategy

In politics, theories are all the knowledge of the whole that one can have. There is no way of controlled experiment and systematic verification to convert theories into tested certainty. The test is in their general plausibility. In the Fifties the key to an understanding of world events was the Cold War. Today, one must grasp the intent and effect of the Soviet policy of "peaceful coexistence" in order to put the pieces of the world jigsaw puzzle together. Like all policies, this one must be understood in its marginal function, i.e. the way in which it tends to change things by adding to, or subtracting from, the previous commitments of the leading nations. In other words, the "coexistence" policy must be seen against the background of the results produced by Cold War tensions: rapid rearmament of the West, including the forced-speed development of thermonuclear weapons and intercontinental missiles; the creation of a system of alliances with the U. S. A. as its center; the proclamation of "massive retaliation" as the U.

S. A.'s policy of deterrence, designed to prevent the Soviet Union from resorting to even conventional aggression; a virtual prohibition of East-West trade; the deployment of U. S. armed forces in a ring around the Soviet Union and China; a general commitment of the West to the proposition that Communism is a world danger comparable to that of Nazism. The design of the "peaceful coexistence" policy is to dismantle this structure of might and the will that sustains it.

It is idle to speculate on the reasons why the Soviets adopted the "peaceful coexistence" policy. They may be negative in the sense that the costs of a potential nuclear war were judged intolerable, or positive in the sense that the usefulness of certain mass psychological factors for the Soviet Union had turned out greater than anticipated. The policy itself was long in the making. Stalin had laid the foundations even before 1950. In 1955 the Soviets used the Austrian Treaty as a dry run and found that it resulted in the Geneva Conference, the first breakthrough of the general isolation of the Communists. Even after the official proclamation of the principle of peaceful coexistence in 1956, the XXI Party Congress, the meeting of 81 Communist parties in November–December 1960, and the XXII Party Congress in 1961 added further details. The new Program of the CPSU adopted at the XXII Congress contains the fullest statement of the policy, complete with all its broad assumptions regarding the political and social forces in the present world situation.

One might say that the policy has sprung from a negative proposition: it eliminated Lenin's and Stalin's assumption that a military showdown between the two world "camps" must be considered inevitable. Thus one could gain the impression that a vacuum had resulted. This is what moves many people to believe that the core resolution of Communism no longer exists, something else moves in to fill its place, and this something else is then believed to consist in our own way of thinking. In reality, though, there is no vacuum. If one looks at Lenin's original theory closely, one finds that it has two aspects. He spoke of the inevitability of war because he considered the world dominated by imperialist powers which could not help wanting to divide and "redivide" the world among themselves. On the other hand, he looked for a violent clash to occur eventually between the forces of revolutionary socialism and those of capitalism so that one of them would sing a "funeral dirge" over the other. Lenin was certain that it would be sung over capitalism. Thus the eventual military showdown would be the occasion on which capitalism would meet its end and a worldwide transition to socialism would begin. All the same, war does not figure in Communist thinking as the chosen means through which to consummate the Revolution. One can find a tendency to this kind of thinking in the writings of Mao Tse-tung, but even there only as an addition to the general Leninist cast of the ideology. A war between the two world "camps," then, was expected rather than designed, and "peaceful coexistence" changes this expectation. Rather than leaving a vacuum, it emphasizes another way of breaking bourgeois political power and setting up regimes of Communists. The other way is officially called "the peaceful transition from capitalism to socialism."

As early as 1872 Marx had spoken of the possibility that

in some countries, notably the United States, open democratic procedures might enable a socialist popular majority
to effect the Revolution through radical laws. Lenin had
declared this early hypothesis of a "democratic" socialist
transformation dated and rendered invalid by subsequent
developments. Under prevailing circumstances, he said,
only force could overthrow the ruling class. His "inevitable war" thesis merely pointed to one most likely situation
in which a forcible overthrow of capitalism could be expected. Khrushchev did not return to the Marx of 1872.
Rather, the new policy was based on the lessons of the
United Front and Popular Front in the Thirties, and the
coalition governments through which Communists obtained control of East European countries in the Forties.
If Lenin's "inevitable war" functioned as a vehicle of radical social change, what other mode of passage from one
society to a new one has taken its place? The new policy
has a key concept spelling out the expectations on which
it rests. Its name is peaceful transition from capitalism to
socialism, and it hinges on a key concept: "radical reforms
short of revolution." To appreciate the importance of this
concept one must remember that Leninism is that branch
of Marxism which always rejected any kinds of reforms on
principle, calling them inadmissible compromises with a
society that must rather be totally destroyed. If Communism now advocates "radical reforms" as something akin
to revolution then it departs in that respect from previous
Leninist teachings. This, at any rate, is how the matter
appears, until one looks closely to see what is meant by
"radical reforms." On that question, the 1961 Party Program leaves no doubt.

"Reform" Communism

Roughly, one finds there three targets for "radical reforms." The first is the dismantlement of all Western resistance to the Soviet Union, in the form of disarmament, weakening or dissolution of the Western alliance system, removal of the military bases surrounding the Soviet Union, and liquidation of "anti-Communism" or the assumption that Communism is a worldwide threat. Secondly, "radical reforms" mean broad and massive nationalization of industries, banks and other key economic positions. Thirdly, something called "broad democracy" is desired, i.e. official and flexible permissiveness for all kinds of protest movements and leftist political mass organizations. What would the Communists hope to accomplish by means of "radical reforms" substituted as a goal "short of revolution"? One can answer this question only in the light of the lessons the Communists learned in the Forties in Eastern Europe. It would seem that "radical reforms" are expected to provide common ground on which the Communists could enter into political alliances with what they call the "progressive elements" of the liberal bourgeoisie, social democrats, the Negro movement, the trade unions, and other political forces enjoying mass support. By way of such alliances and common causes the Communists would then hope to make their way into the government of the United States or other Western countries, presumably as coalition partners. Once in power, they would expect to "launch a broad mass struggle outside parliament, smash the resistance of the reactionary forces, and provide the necessary conditions for a peaceful socialist revolution" (1961 Program of the CPSU, Part One, V). In other

words, the Communists, no longer counting on an overthrow of capitalism by a revolutionary upheaval of the
masses, seek above all to obtain a measure of control of
governmental public power as members of a political
movement dedicated to "radical reforms," so that they can
turn this power to the destruction of their enemies and
thus carry out "revolution from above." Since violence
against the enemies of the revolution would be practiced
by the government and the Communists would hope to
enter the government by invitation of their coalition partners, they call the entire process "peaceful transition to
socialism." They hasten to add that if the "ruling classes"
do not cooperate the "proletariat must break their resistance by civil war."

The new policy has an indispensable international dimension: the so-called "national liberation movement." In
the speech in which Khrushchev ruled out the "inevitability of war," he distinguished four categories of war: "world
wars, local wars, national liberation wars, and popular
uprisings" (speech of January 6, 1961). Communists, he
added, are opposed to world wars and local wars, but have
"a most positive attitude" toward national liberation wars
and popular uprisings. It is significant that he classified the
latter under the broad category of "wars." In other words,
while the Soviets would avoid all-out nuclear war and even
what Western strategists call "brushfire wars" between
themselves and Western countries, they would seek to
embroil the West in wars conducted, not between states,
but rather by irregular forces, allegedly insurrectionist
movements, and fought for the sake of supposedly justified
causes such as "national liberation" and "people's indignation" over social conditions. It is a characteristic feature

of these wars that the danger of their escalation into "world wars" can always be made to loom up as the risk attached to the West's attempt to win the contest. As the West becomes involved in such wars, the Soviet Union could hope to find an increasingly favorable disposition among the "progressive elements" of the Western population for appeals based on anti-imperialism, anti-militarism, and anti-war sentiments. Thus these wars would open up fissures in the West which would eventually greatly increase the Communists' chances to enter into a coalition with pacifists, democratic progressivists, social democrats, and other political movements, all of whom would provide the mass support to help the Communists attain positions of public power.

It is well worthwhile to look a little closer at the components of the new policy.

Covert Wars

Our language has no name for armed conflict that employs military force but is not war between states or governments, combines the use of force with political activity designed to intimidate, paralyze, and decompose the opponent's social fabric, aims at conquest but knows no visible front lines, turns on concrete objectives which all the same have little if anything to do with the underlying conflict. There is no precedent for this kind of war. It has appeared in our times from a combination of Communist ideology and worldwide organization, the atomic stalemate, the ongoing process of decolonization, and the potentiality of widespread discontents that can be whipped into frenzied mass psychoses. A European expert has suggested the term "covert war," something between hot and cold war, between civil and international war, between a contest of force and political manipulation. There are concrete objectives at stake, possibly a piece of territory, or control of a given government. At the same time, though, intangible objectives are added; for instance, to loosen or shake the enemy's social fabric, to undermine certain policies or the mind and will that conceived them, to create or unmake certain moods. Covert war can be fought to the point of local victory or simply peter out. It can range from scattered guerilla operations to clashes between forces of division size, with mass rioting, assassination, international conferences, and propaganda campaigns thrown in. Violence and political operations always combine for total effect, none of them has independent ends. Political methods include infiltration, subversion, terror, threats, promises, negotiations, repeated emotional shocks, the stirring up of self-doubts and guilt feelings in the opponent, promotion of a widespread sense of crisis and insecurity. Among the methods of violence are sabotage, guerilla and partisan warfare, assassination, insurrection, civil war, and open force conducted by covert, i.e. irregularly employed, units. As far as the West is concerned, states are involved on one side, while the other side is elusive, fading away and then reappearing, neither having political structure nor being wholly shapeless.

The importance of each of such conflicts is divided between the immediate and local issue and the indirect and global effects. The mighty forces of a great power will appear locked in battle with a half-visible enemy that can be passed off as a small people or heroic insurrectionist movement seeking justice or national liberty. If the great power accepts what appears as defeat, it will suffer a tremendous loss of prestige with friend and foe alike, and in all probability also succumb to a mood of national depression. Further operations against it will not be countered with either the determination or the international support as before. If superior in the field, the great power becomes subject to the charge of brutality and aggression. By its inevitable association with a local government, in an area that probably has never known democracy or even good government before, the local regime can be made to appear tyrannous or even "fascist." The fighting presence of Western forces in overseas areas of former colonies can be made to support the accusation of "imperialism." It is relatively easy to make the immediate issue appear remote, unimportant, and unrelated to national security considerations, and thus to characterize the fighting as sheer militaristic aggression. What is more, covert wars do not admit of any clear-cut victory. For whatever can be said of war as international anarchy, it usually occurs against a background of international consensus in which war functions as an arbiter regarding the relative rank of nations, so that a defeated nation understands that in defeat it has been taken quite a few notches down, not to speak of the inevitable losses in territory and wealth. Where war occurs, not between states but between a state and irregular forces, there is no criterion for victory in the conventional sense. On the part of the state, victory would mean the end of irregular operations, but there is no government that could or would guarantee such an end, nor could any negotiations be considered conclusive. On the part of the irregular forces, the opponents' political exhaustion or loss of prestige would be victory, but this again

is not something measurable in terms of a treaty. For the
"insurrectionists" or "liberation forces," to obtain control
over territory or a government is, of course, a clear-cut
local victory, but in the global balance of the conflict this
too eludes the conventional classification of a war's end.
Thus such wars tend to go on, whether or not there have
been negotiations, or even treaties. No formal "peace" can
guarantee their cessation, since their causes are not local
or even truly represented by the local issue, but they may
die down, at least for a while, without any kind of agreement.

Covert wars tend to produce profound tensions both
within and among Western nations. The fighting that
seems endless will grate on political nerves. The distance
of the war's theater will prevent any mobilization of a
national sense of danger. Statesmen will become unsure of
themselves under the burden of public disapproval.
Domestic opposition to such wars will take on overtones
of a basic social criticism ("a society in which this kind of
thing is possible," . . .) and the government will have to
defend the war against a revolutionary mood, so that the
opposing arguments do not meet on the same level. The
most powerful nation is thus compelled to face political
corrosion at home and abroad without being able to retali-
ate in kind. One can easily see why Communists maintain
"a most positive attitude" toward "wars of national liberation and popular uprisings," the Soviet term for covert
wars in the age of atomic stalemate.

The ultimate purpose of covert wars must be sought, not
in the local advances they make possible, but in the political developments within Western countries. The Communists always seek to attach large masses to their leadership

to provide the numerical support that they cannot obtain directly for themselves. They know that they have frightened the world so deeply that only small minorities are likely to respond to the appeal of their ideology. The power of mass support can be theirs only on the ground of "common causes" in which non-Communists can be induced to join with Communists. It was Lenin who first conceived this device of enlarging the power base of a numerically small and weak "vanguard" party. Communists, he said, must present themselves as "tribunes of the people," champions of all kinds of grievances, discontents, and complaints. If we remember that at the same time he denounced the "spontaneity" of the people as "reactionary" and "bourgeois" we understand that Communists are not meant to commit themselves chiefly to the redress of actual injustices, but rather to use partial and concrete dissatisfactions in order to meld them into one single and universal dissatisfaction with everything that is, against which Communists would be the sole and effective champions. Later, Communists hit upon a few widely appealing "common causes," all rooted in the liberal way of thinking with its ideological visions of progress, equality, enduring peace. On these foundations they established their United Fronts, Popular Fronts, coalitions, national-democratic fronts, and working-class alliances.

Communist Coalition Politics

The universal condemnation of Fascism or Nazism, for instance, is one of the great political realities of our time. Even though Stalin's cooperation with Hitler made World War II possible, the Soviets now draw major political capital from their historic role as Fascism's conquerors. If they had been the sole enemies of Fascism they could unquestionably claim to be the antipode to a universally feared evil. Unfortunately for them, there were others who had an even better claim to that title: the forces of political liberty, those of Christianity, the protagonists of human dignity, the Western democracies. In reality, though, the situation is complex in the extreme, from freedom-loving Finland's alliance with Hitler and the wholly ambiguous situation in Yugoslavia to the differences between Hitler and Mussolini, not to speak of Franco who does not fit into either of these patterns. Complex situations do not lend themselves to the formulation of broad "common causes" that have to be reduced to simplistic formulae capable of serving as the cement for broad political "fronts." The Communists, therefore, seek above all to simplify and polarize the pertinent political imagery. In brief, they are interested in identifying their present opponents with Fascism and passing themselves off as the sole, original, and only genuine anti-Fascists. This intent is behind their insistent charges that the U. S. A. now operates as the "world gendarme," the hateful "cop," in alliance with "Fascist" regimes all over the world, and by means of "Fascist aggression." Along another line, they identify the bombing of Hiroshima and Dresden during World War II with the Nazi atrocities of Buchenwald, Dachau, and Auschwitz, establishing a kind of symmetry of wrongs in which the wrong on one side can at any time be exchanged for the wrong of the other. At the time when German rearmament within NATO finally became effective, a wave of anti-German films suddenly appeared in the West's major cities. About the same time, Hochhuth's *Der Stellvertreter*

(The Deputy) seemed to identify the Pope with Fascist and Nazi atrocities. Such developments made it possible for the Communists to insinuate that the United States and the Catholic hierarchy were fundamentally on the same side, or of the same character, as Fascism, not only for the present period but for the decisive time of World War II. To the extent to which this hint takes effect, the Communists emerge in the public eye as the only honest foes of Fascism. A further and similar propaganda operation now seeks to fasten the Fascist label on any kind of anti-Communism. In Communist documents, the two terms are very nearly used as synonyms, suggesting that there could be no other ground on which one would combat Communism than that of Fascist leanings. In other words, all these attempts seek to reduce the various opponents of Communism to a single category, one whose evil is never doubted: Fascism, with militarism thrown in for good measure. So far, this operation has netted the Soviets astonishing gains. There are many who never before thought of evil as a reality but came to accept the reality of Fascist evil in the Thirties, to whom this kind of thinking appeals very much. They now are disposed to fight anti-Communism in the Free World as a political danger greater than Communism, who even today look to the right as the sole possible threat of dictatorship, who think of governments like those of Chiang Kai-shek, President Thieu, and Premier Vorster as the worst political evil that could befall a nation, while saving for the Soviets their most fervent hopes of peace and harmony, whose leading principle is *"pas d'ennemi à gauche"* and "the enemy is always on the right."

The fear of atomic war is another of the facts of contemporary political life on which the Communists try to establish a "common cause." According to its own ideology, Communism is not pacifistic. It assumes the probability of war, preaches the virtue of first-rate armaments, and the vigilance of preparedness. In 1949, however, the year in which the Soviet Union produced its first atomic bomb and the capacity for atomic blackmail, Stalin organized the first "peace campaign" beginning with an international conference in Stockholm and a worldwide circulation of a list of signatures for peace. Since then the Soviets have never ceased to advance disarmament proposals which are more of a political than a military-effective type: for instance, global condemnations of aggression, resolutions outlawing atomic weapons but without establishing inspection. When the United States, on the other hand, presented the Baruch Plan to put atomic weapons and production under international control and then to abolish them, the Soviets immediately turned it down. In their propaganda they have stressed to the point of distortion the unimaginable evil of atomic war, and on the other dazzled before the eyes of a frightened world the prospect of universal disarmament without ever making a practical contribution thereto. Peace, war, and disarmament are themes used chiefly to the end of weakening the political nerves of the Free World. In the same way, the Soviets have used international crises and covert wars to stir up acute fears of an imminent atomic catastrophe, through which they have put the mortgage of threatened "escalation" on any ongoing covert war. The term "escalation" already conjures up an irresistible motion toward the "ultimate evil" and has been used to hamstring the Western will to fight to win. Beyond this, Communist propaganda has tried to link the evil of nuclear war with the nature of

Western society in an attempt to turn pacifism into a revolutionary cause. Some American civil rights organizations have added the issue of war in general and nuclear war in particular to their otherwise purely domestic concerns. As we noted above, the Communist propaganda aims at representing each fear, each discontent, each complaint as merely an aspect of a general rejection of the entire society. That is the meaning of the endeavor to reduce several enemies of Communism to one enemy, several evils to one general evil, and to have Communism appear as the one Galahad doing battle against that one evil. In the words of the 1961 Program of the CPSU:

> Socialist revolutions, anti-imperialist national liberation revolutions, people's democratic revolutions, broad peasant movements, popular struggles to overthrow Fascist and other despotic regimes, and general democratic movements against national oppression—all these merge in a single revolutionary process undermining and destroying capitalism.

"Common causes" are not ends in themselves. They serve a double purpose. On the one hand, they are supposed to pry loose entire chunks of Western population from their traditional moorings and cast them politically adrift; on the other hand, the Communist Party stands ready to provide leadership and apparent reintegration to the disoriented. This latter purpose, however, requires organization. The translation of "common causes" into an organizational structure provides for the Communist Party a role not as nominal boss but rather as an apparently *bona fide* partner in a fellowship, be it named "alliance," "coalition," "United Front," "Popular Front," "Democratic

Front," "Progressive Front," the "New Left," or some other appropriate phrase.

Uses of Mass Organizations

After World War II the Communists adopted a pattern of peaceful conquest that has made use of four types of organization: Special purpose organizations, broad mass organizations, roof organizations, and new political parties. Special purpose organizations form around particular causes, as, for instance, nuclear disarmament, civil rights, some particular case of injustice—causes, in other words, which have nothing to do with Communist objectives but represent at least a partial indictment of society. Those most valuable to Communist ends form without Communist instigation but have a revolutionary potential. Some endure for a considerable time, others rise and fall like meteors. Trade unions are the most lasting of these special purpose organizations. They have always been considered a favorable Communist hunting ground, even though the unions themselves have often been extremely effective in keeping Communists off their premises. In spite of the strong anti-Communist record of most American unions, Gus Hall emphasized the importance Communists attribute to organized labor as the key to their efforts among various organizations. To labor must be added, as a special windfall, the "New Left," consisting, in Communist terms, of the "radicalized intelligentsia" and the "radicalized youth." Particular organizations fluctuate; some, like the DuBois Clubs, the Students for a Democratic Society (SDS), SNCC, SANE, provide a more permanent center around which others appear and disappear, but even these centers are subject to periodic regroupments. Overlapping these, the various organizations of the civil rights movement stretch out in a fairly broad spectrum. It would be a mistake to consider all or some of these associations Communist branch offices. Many consist of radical romantics who are unusable for Communist discipline. Nor does their value to Communists consist in anything like organized and reliable control of membership or votes. These associations are able, though, to agitate, to increase a state of confusion, disorganization, and instability, and to create a general impression that the social order is coming to an end and that "something new" must be embraced.

Communist mass organizations play a similarly vague auxiliary role. They aim to yank previously stirred-up people from their quiescence by organizing them, probably for the first time in their lives, on a large scale that creates the impression of great importance. Youth organizations, organizations of women, organizations of small businessmen, of the poor, or in other big categories can excite in people vague but "great expectations" without necessarily committing them to any particular goal or action. Such mass organizations constitute something like a potential, ready to be converted into actual power when a sudden crisis arises. It takes only a few Communists in key positions, particularly in the propaganda machinery of such organizations, to actualize their power which, however, is never decisive. Next, the Communists seem to feel the need for large "roof organizations" to hold particular organizations together in some vague fashion. Such roof organizations can be established in a particular country or on an international scale. In a particular country they may be set up as organizations of the unity of the working class, or democratic or antifascist unity. Internationally, hostility to imperialism or the fear of atomic war may serve as the banner. The World Peace Movement functioned for a while as a roof organization. International Youth Conferences still play that role. In January 1966 the so-called Tri-Continental Conference at Havana brought diverse elements together in an attempt to unite them for a common purpose and to gain their support for a modicum of common action.

The types of organizations so far mentioned are all loose, effective more through agitation than organized control, purposely imprecise in their aims, and not subject to "Communist discipline." In other words, they operate as nets in which to catch and hold mass support. The Communists know, however, that in politics it is indispensable to have the effective command structure of a party organization, particularly the type of party they have in mind. Also, they do not delude themselves about their chance to take over already existing parties with long established traditions. Thus they have a paramount interest in founding a new party among the masses whom their agitation has loosened up and excited politically. This is the pattern they followed in Eastern Europe. Now they are ready to apply it to the United States. In 1966 the CPUSA adopted a new Program that among other things calls for the formation of a "new people's party" drawn "from the forces arrayed against monopoly: the Negro people, independent farmers, intellectuals, professionals, small businessmen and other middle strata; youth and other groups." "Monopoly" is a broad term that can be used to cover any kind of discontent with the extant society. The new party, the Program continues, is to aim at reforms that will "weaken monopoly, "enhance the self-confidence, strength, unity and fighting capacity of the working class and its allies," and change the foreign and military policy of the U. S. A. The domestic application of the global strategy of Soviet Communism is here spelled out, although in terms of the Communist jargon that are clear only to the initiated. What is most significant is that the new party is not meant to replace or absorb the Communist Party. The latter would supposedly enter the new party but remain independent, as a tightly knit and disciplined cadre organization, a command unit within a larger command unit within a larger command structure, disposing of countless means to stir up the masses, promote divisions and antagonisms, pushing the entire society toward a crisis in which the new party, with the CPUSA at its center, would appear as the only stable point, the sole means of unity.

The Road to Power?

We could do worse than to look at a paper read on April 28, 1966, by Professor Herbert Marcuse, a Marxist, who, after admitting that the main tenets of Marx have all been refuted by history, then asked what could be done to "save Marx's concept." Having specifically discounted the possibility of a proletarian revolution in Western industrialized countries, he then spelled out a way by which "Marx's concept" could be "saved": through a combination of a) the national liberation struggle in the backward countries; b) the mass parties of the working class of the West, particularly of Italy and France, "operating under the new strategy"; c) the underprivileged elements within the

Western industrialized countries (obviously Negroes, mainly); and d) the "radicalized intelligentsia and radicalized youth." Of these four, to which he added the "communist-controlled countries" as a fifth factor, the most important ones, he said, were the "national liberation struggle" and the "radicalized intelligentsia and radicalized youth." (*Marx and the Western World*, ed. by N. Lobkowicz, Notre Dame Univ. Press, 1967) One can readily recognize in this statement the pattern of the "new strategy" with its covert wars, common causes, coalitions and alliances, mass agitation, and new parties. What is remarkable is that this strategy is the first one in Communist history to envisage a chain of engagements and developments designed to lead all the way to a Communist takeover in the leading countries of the West. In this sense, there has never been what many people like to call a "blueprint of world conquest" by Communism. On two previous occasions, the Communists have elaborated grand strategic designs. The first of these was produced at the VI World Congress in 1928 and the second at the VII World Congress in 1935. Both of these, however, limited themselves to an assessment of world forces and some guiding principles for Communist conflict management, principles meant to remain binding for a period of a number of years. Neither plan, however, indicated just how these principles could or would lead the Communist forces to final victory. "Peaceful coexistence," elaborated from 1956 to 1961, is the first plan to map a possible road all the way to Communist control of mighty Western countries. These countries, particularly the U. S. A., will be involved in wars in backward areas against apparently helpless and backward peoples. That involvement will be publicly and globally attacked as imperialistic, militaristic, fascist, and criminal. Strong forces of domestic opposition to these involvements will emerge in the West to join the Communist chorus. They will converge on objectives like "ending the Cold War," "disarmament," and radical social change at home. As a radicalized movement gathers momentum, it cannot be deemed impossible for a vast network of radical organizations, wheels within wheels, to elbow out one of the great traditional parties, particularly in a mood of crisis. Such a movement would, among other things, be spurred on by the hope that the Communists, in joining, were about to become respectable, apparent partners in civilization and peace, which in turn would promise an end of international tensions and the Cold War. Hopes and fears combined could well engender a strong political momentum. The Communists might be accepted as members of a broad coalition and ride on its coattails into both houses of Congress, and particularly into important positions in the bureaucracy. Important policy decisions would be contemplated as concessions to the Communist coalition partners, among them a treaty outlawing nuclear weapons and storing existing ones in mothballs. East-West trade would be thrown wide open. American troops at European and Asian bases would be reduced or recalled. The Communists would then seek to cash in on the capital of the "common cause" by demanding that certain groups or individuals be branded as "unpatriotic" or "undemocratic" or "nonpeaceloving," and be removed or politically curtailed. By such procedures they would hope to paralyze or destroy anti-Communism. If their aims or methods were to arouse the suspicion of their coalition partners, the Communists might appeal directly to "the

people," launching the previously created mass organizations into the street to demonstrate the "people's" will.
Even allowing the most favorable circumstances, from the
Communist point of view, there is no question that in a
country like the United States the Communists would face
an enormously difficult task and could expect to move
ahead only by inches. All the same, once the Communists
could enjoy and invoke for themselves the legitimacy of a
widely accepted "common cause" and under the protec-
tion of this label move into the government, only open
civil violence could deter or dislodge them.

This is obviously what Communist planning now believes possible and feasible. One need not accept the Communist expectation as an assurance that things will
develop in this manner. All the same, it would be extremely shortsighted to take our own immunity from
Communist seduction and pressure for granted. Beyond
that, one should realize that the entire policy of "peaceful
coexistence" rests on the assumption of an equilibrium of
military forces and a balance of deterrence. Even if
"peaceful coexistence" were not to culminate in an inclusion of Communists in a ruling coalition, and if it achieved
nothing more than the removal of the deterrence that now
bars Soviet expansion, it would constitute an enormous
gain for the Soviets. After that the Communists, secure in
the indisturbable control of one third of the globe, could,
and in all probability would, pass on to another strategy,
one that no longer included the elimination of "world
war."

CHAPTER 8

The Sino-Soviet Split

The rift between the two major power centers of the Communist world has figured hugely in the policy decisions of the leading powers. As a fact of contemporary world politics, it ranks second only to nuclear arms. It has stimulated more wishful thinking in the West than even de-Stalinization itself. This should not obscure the very great importance of the rift, but should rather lead to greater efforts to think through the implications of this fact, soberly, critically, and realistically.

Mao's Orthodoxy

Before 1949, the relation of the Chinese Communist Party to Moscow was that of a powerless satellite. It is not true that Mao Tse-tung developed a Marxist heresy against Soviet resistance. The heresy is supposed to consist in reliance on the peasantry as the main force of a Communist revolution. That, indeed, was Mao's strategy. But Mao did not come to the fore in the Chinese Communist Party until the end of 1927. A year earlier, the Executive Committee of the Comintern in Moscow had decided that the Chinese revolution was in its "agrarian phase," and in September 1927 Stalin had authoritatively laid down the peasant line for China and called for the immediate formation of "rural Soviets" in China. The concept goes back to Lenin's thought about revolutionary strategy, as formulated in 1905 and 1906, and reiterated, with particular emphasis on Asia, in 1920. This was not the first or last time that Moscow prescribed and the Chinese Communists heeded the Leninist-Stalinist conception of revolution in China. In 1935 the order came from on high for the Chinese Communists to form a United Front with the Kuomintang, and again in 1944 Moscow dictated a coalition policy which at that time coincided with official American ideas on how to handle the Chinese problem. During the long period in which the Communists were holed up in Yenan, they depended on Soviet support for arms and money. After the end of World War II, when Stalin seemed to have counted on a long period of coalition politics and accordingly concluded a treaty with Chiang Kai-shek, he still barred Chiang's armies from Southern Manchuria and turned over the stores of captured Japanese arms to Mao's forces, thus enabling Mao to turn the tide in the civil war. In other words, it is not in the pre-1949 period that the present conflict originated.

Stalin may have had his special reasons for wishing the Chinese Communists in a coalition rather than as sole rulers of the country. Communist regimes are committed to accelerated industrialization. China in 1949 was a country far less industrialized than Russia had been in 1917. The costs of industrializing China would be staggering, and Stalin expressed to Averell Harriman his fears that a Communist China might well bleed Russia to death. When Stalin extended aid to Communist China in 1950, the first aid the Soviet Union granted to another country, it was a very small loan: $300 million. Four years later an additional credit of $130 million came forth. The Soviet Union committed itself to build 65 industrial plants for China, then 91 more, then still more. In 1957 Russia promised to build an atomic plant in China. Betwen 10,000 and 20,000 Soviet technicians went to China to supervise these projects. Thousands of young Chinese were trained at Russian universities. The treaty of friendship and alliance which Russia concluded with Mao in 1950, thereby superseding the 1945 treaty with Chiang Kai-shek, promised among other things the return of the Changchun Railway and Port Arthur within a specified period, which was later extended. All this fell considerably short of what the Chinese wanted. China's needs were far greater than those of already industrialized Europe, but Soviet aid to China was far less than U.S. aid to any of the leading European nations.

Disagreements on Policy

To these disappointments and grievances were added disagreements over de-Stalinization. The condemnation of Stalin and reversal of some of his policies concerned the entire Communist world, but it was decided within the Kremlin, and Mao had not been consulted. The Chinese press continued to praise Stalin after such praise had disappeared from the Soviet press. The Chinese eventually fell in line with de-Stalinization and even "peaceful coexistence," but with manifest reservations. These tensions flared into open disagreement when Khrushchev, in December 1958, sharply criticized the introduction of "people's communes" into China. When he denounced the communes as "reactionary" he may have been prompted not only by ideological but also by economic worries. The communes resembled the disastrous policy adopted by the Soviet government which is usually misnamed "war communism," and which brought the entire Russian economy to collapse. If something similar happened to Communist China, Russia obviously would have to foot the bill.

To Khrushchev's attack on their domestic policy the Chinese Communists replied with an attack on Khrushchev's foreign policy. Their motives may again have consisted of a typical mixture of ideological and power considerations, the latter stemming from the Kremlin's aloof attitude during the 1959 Sino-Indian border clash, which, moreover, coincided with a withdrawal of the Soviet promise for a Chinese atomic plant. At this point, the Chinese launched their attack in the form of a purely ideological argument, in a series of articles entitled "Long Live Leninism," April 1960. From then on, the dispute began to feed on its own heat. Later in 1960, the Soviet technicians left China. Soviet trade with China began to decline and China's trade with non-Communist countries, at first Canada and Australia, began to pick up, until at present less than 40 percent of Chinese trade is with the Communist bloc. In typical Communist fashion, the mutual recriminations quickly reached superlatives of denunciatory bitterness. The Soviets charge the Chinese with "dogmatism" or "adventurism," the Chinese blamed the Russians for "revisionism" or "capitulism." Moscow blamed Peking for sabotaging the war in Vietnam, Peking accused Moscow of complicity with the imperialists.

It is obvious that the quarrel would not have taken this bitter form if both sides had not invoked an obligation to a common cause and a common principle which they believed the other side had betrayed. Thus in the midst of antagonism and recrimination both sides know and proclaim that the rift should not exist. We may recall the precedent of Tito, who was expelled from the Cominform, called an "agent of imperialism," and actually threatened with invasion of his country. Even in this moment of danger, though, Tito never felt that he could join the West, and declared to a Western journalist that in the event of a world war he would fight on the side of the Soviet Union. Both he and the Kremlin rulers obviously never ceased looking on the separation as an anomaly. Eventually a reconciliation took place and, while Tito has not surrendered his divergent views, he is fully accepted in the family fold again.

The quarrel between Chinese and Russian Communists differs only in one respect from other policy quarrels that have from time to time occurred in Communist ranks: when there are differences within a single party, there is machinery through which to settle the dispute and restore unity. The conflict between Trotsky and Stalin was in no way less bitter than that between Moscow and Peking, but there existed institutions and procedures that enabled Stalin to gain a clear-cut victory and to expel Trotsky not only from the Party but also from the entire Communist movement. As long as international Communism was administered by the Soviet government, differences between Communists anywhere in the world could be settled definitively. Thus, for instance, the fight between Lovestone and Browder in the CPUSA was decided by Stalin in favor of Browder, who had only minority support, but who thenceforth was certified as the sole representative of legitimate Communism in the United States. Tito's Yugoslavia was the first case of a country in which a Communist party, coming to power, disposed of its own machinery of terror and enforcement and did not owe its ascendancy to the Soviets. When a difference of opinion arose, it could therefore not be settled by pressure or intimidation: Tito had a certain amount of autonomous security. The Chinese Communists won control over the whole of China after having fought a long civil war and also administered a certain amount of territory independently. They were equipped with armed forces and administrative cadres far better than the Russian Communists were in 1917. Moscow still enjoyed authority as the "most advanced socialist country" and as the party of Lenin, but it did not have the means to impose its decisions on recalcitrant Communist parties who had their own police and party control. Under those circumstances, the Leninist disposition to "split," i.e. drive each argument to the point of its most extreme formulation and to widen each fissure into a break, would necessarily create something like an international conflict, and Communists have not nurtured a tradition of compromise on such matters. In the late Fifties, an attempt was made to set up something like a Communist world council. A number of Communist parties met in 1957, more met in 1960, and both Moscow and Peking declared the pronouncements of these gatherings "binding." The procedure, however, remained ineffective, as both sides simply accused each other later of having deviated from these "binding" resolutions. All the same, Communism is predicated on the assumption that there can be only one correct Party line. Thus both sides, in their desire to restore this unity, claim superior authority, Russia by virtue of being "most advanced" on the road to Communism, China by virtue of Mao's greater seniority and merit as a theoretician.

A Common Ideology

In the sense in which the Communists speak of an "ideological struggle" between the bourgeoisie and Communism, there is no quarrel between Moscow and Peking. Both agree on the world view created by Marx and the main lines of revolutionary strategy built into the ideology by Lenin. Both look for, and dedicate themselves to, the overthrow of "imperialism," i.e. the free world. The world, their enemy, and they themselves appear to all Communists in the same perspective. This common outlook furnishes the basis for the mutual accusations of deviation, betrayal, and dereliction of duty. Such accusations are hurled in the course of differences over concrete policies and courses of action in their mutual relationship as well as in relation to the common enemy. In the Communist world, ideological differences are always power conflicts, and all power conflicts invariably take on an ideological character. It is not possible to speak of an ideological conflict that would remain purely in the realm of intellectual contention, nor can one find among Communists power rivalry or power plays that have no ideological significance. One of the power factors stems from the Soviet Union's greater economic wealth, and China's great economic needs. This difference has also been translated into ideological terms, the Chinese calling the Soviet Union one of the "city" countries of the world, together with the imperialist nations, and grouping themselves with the "countryside," i.e. the have-nots. Another power factor resides in the capacity of China as well as the Soviet Union to make foreign policy and to wage war. This is a novelty. In the past no Communist country outside the Soviet Union could have a foreign policy of its own, and all Communist armed forces with the exception of Tito's were effectively under Soviet command. Communist foreign policy is also Communist revolutionary strategy; the Communist mind can never separate the relations of a Communist-controlled country with other countries from the ideological purposes of his movement. To the extent to which the foreign policy of Communist China differs from Soviet conceptions, the Chinese create circumstances that will become binding on the Soviet Union whether the Kremlin likes it or not. The charge of "capitulism" (withdrawing under pressure, as in the case of Cuba) can be repeated effectively each time the Soviet Union refuses to participate actively in a revolutionist venture the Chinese may have started. On the other hand, the Soviet Union has gone quite far in its endeavor to regain its independence from this bothersome partnership. At any rate, Chinese national security is no longer guaranteed by the same kind of Soviet commitment that the U. S. A. still acknowledges with regard to Western Europe.

On the other hand, the Chinese Communists, like Stalin in 1941, have sought to identify Chinese nationalism with their leadership and cause. In China's case, this has amounted to a drive to regain all territories ceded to foreign powers under the so-called "unequal treaties" which were imposed on a weak China by incomparably stronger "imperialist" powers. In this perspective, Communism is made to appear as a movement to restore China's territorial integrity, one of the "causes" to which wide masses who are not persuaded of the Communist iedology will nevertheless give their fervent support. Chinese maps have long claimed as Chinese considerable areas now under Soviet control. Armed clashes between Chinese and Soviet forces on the Ussuri and Amur rivers and in Singkiang have served to dramatize these claims. Pictures of troops thus killed by the other side have been used by the propaganda machinery of both sides to whip up popular sentiment of indignation and anticipation of possible war. Anybody familiar with Communist propaganda operations knows that Communist regimes do not operate in response to public opinion, to which they attribute no authority whatever, but do use the appearance of public opinion to justify certain measures and policies in the eyes of the world. There has been considerable and justified speculation whether the proclamation of the Brezhnev doctrine in the fall of 1968 served the same purpose. It came too late to underpin the occupation of Czechoslovakia with a foundation of apparent righteousness, but while it could glaze over that invasion only ex post facto, it could be used as a title for future intervention in China. Such Communist maneuvers are usually political-psychological, indicating resolve and sternness, hinting at dire possibilities, invoking revolutionary duty and socialist authority, and seeking to intimidate the other side. In the Sino-Soviet conflict, both sides have proceeded in this fashion. The border clashes have remained examples rather than decisive actions. The Soviet Union has established a Central Asian command and somewhat reinforced its troops there, but its deployment is still far short of any realistic preparation for major war with China. The shooting incidents were conveniently followed by talks, after which not only the shooting but also the mutual recriminations eased. Again, this should not be mistaken as a final accommodation, but rather as a power maneuver in a situation where the common Communist ideology has not produced any machinery to settle disputes between "fraternal" parties. As for the prospects of a real down-to-the-bitter-end war between the Soviet Union and China, one should always remember what the leaders of both regimes undoubtedly recall every waking minute, that after one of them ended up totally vanquished, the other one, seriously weakened from the contest, would then face the entire Western world alone.

The most interesting aspect of the Sino-Soviet rift lies, however, not in the causes but in the potential effects of this situation. Western observers are too prone to believe that these effects will be confined to the Communist world and that we, the West, are in the position of bystanders who can afford to look on unconcernedly and to intervene at most where intervention will redound to our benefit. In reality, though, the Sino-Soviet rift affects the West as much as the Communists, so that we must learn coolly to appraise the ways in which we, too, are part of this situation.

As early as 1956, Togliatti (then leader of the Italian Communist Party) invented a term which has manifested almost magic powers of hypnosis: polycentrism. Since then, even many well-informed experts have begun to talk not of Communism but of communisms, no longer of

Marxism-Leninism but of Marxism, Leninism, Stalinism, Khrushchevism, Maoism, Titoism, as if these were wholly differing isms—or separate and opposed views of, and purposes in, the world. Actually, the questions of power centers and of different ideologies do not necessarily coincide, as we have seen. If asked about the content of the Communist ideology, answers in Moscow and in Peking would tend to be identical, and differences would show up only if one asked which of the two centers had remained loyal to the ideology. One should further distinguish between Communist power centers and centers of Communist authority. Moscow, Peking, and Belgrade are now power centers with some degree of independence, but only the first two have also been acclaimed as centers of authority. Tito, for all his ambition, has not succeeded in his attempt to rival Moscow as the leader of some variety of world Communism.

From 1949 on Moscow and Peking were partners in a Communist "axis," even though, as in the case of the Fascist-Nazi "axis," one side outweighed other. The fact that they considered each other, and were considered by the world, as partners, has lent to their differences the character of a "split," and the split now confronts Communisms all over the world with the need to take sides.

Disunity and Its Effects

In many countries, two or more Communist groups now exist side by side, differing from each other in terms of allegiance or affiliation, as well as of Communist strategy. Among the parties in power some, particularly the Rumanian CP, have used the opportunity to obtain a certain amount of tactical elbowroom for themselves, a kind of local autonomy within the Communist movement. Others, under the strain of necessity, have found that this kind of position was not tenable for long, as they had to make a clear choice between Moscow and Peking. Castro is a case in point. It was his exposed position, in which only Moscow's highly developed military power could protect him, which forced his hand. At the same time one should note that precisely the Rumanian Communists, having launched a qualified Declaration of Party Independence, have been most unhappy over the quarrel that allowed them to do so and have strongly urged the restoration of world Communist unity. Even while enjoying their limited autonomy, they have not ceased being Communists and have wielded their totalitarian rule for the sake of ideological objectives.

In the absence of any machinery for the settling of politico-ideological disputes, there is little likelihood that the differences between Moscow and Peking will go away. Should Mao Tse-tung be succeeded by a more pro-Soviet group in the CPC, there may well be a grand reconciliation which, however, will not alter the fact that there are two centers capable of deciding authoritatively on questions of Communist policy and incapable of coordinating these decisions so that no rift will emerge. Only a clear and overwhelming preponderance of power would be able to tip the balance in favor of one of these centers, but in view of the nuclear capability of China and her now independent trade relations there is little chance that the Soviet Union will ever be able to establish an overwhelming preponderance of power within a partnership relation. Thus the lack of coordination of decisions made in Moscow and

China will continue, no matter how strongly both sides may wish there were no rift between them. A number of potential developments can be expected within the Communist camp: a) As in the case of Communist parties in other countries, the Communist parties in Soviet Russia and China may also develop split personalities. In either country there may grow up a Soviet as well as a Chinese faction, and these factions may develop such strength that their dispute may not be soluble short of a civil war. In other words, the Party machinery in the leading Communist countries may lose its power to restore its own unity, a power which all the leading Communist parties have hitherto cherished as their greatest source of strength. b) As factional fights continue to fester within the Party of each leading Communist country, the weaker faction within one Party may well apppeal to the Communist Party of the other country for help. Such help will be given, because the outcome of the factional struggle in each Communist Party is of the greatest importance not only to the other Party but to all Communists in the world. The form of help is likely to follow the Communist pattern of infiltration, underground operations, clandestine military and financial aid, and oblique measures of power pressure set up behind some innocent-looking façade. c) For a while, a leading Communist party may succeed in keeping factional fights within its own ranks hidden from the public. After a while, however, the quarrel will come out into the open, and at that point it may well be that the quarreling Communists will begin to appeal to the judgment of the people. So far, Communists have acknowledged accountability only to their own co-ideologists, the "people" for them being beset by the lingering influences

and habits of the "present-day society." An appeal to the
people could not help but having far-reaching consequences for Communist Party rule. The people as an authority is a democratic rather than a Communist concept;
this authority would pronounce its verdict in terms of the
principles of morality, the interests of the living generation, and the continuing affection for the tradition of living. d) Not only factions within a leading Communist
party, but also the two leading Communist parties themselves may try to settle their quarrel by appealing to some
higher judgment. So far, this higher judgment has been the
world Communist movement alone. Appeal to this authority, however, already signifies an important reversal of
previous positions. Formerly the Communist movement
was dependent on the Party line worked out by a small
circle of leaders. Now the leaders and the Party line may
have to bow to the judgment of the rank and file, at least
of Party cadres, without being able to manipulate its support from above. One should not rush to the conclusion,
however, that the rivalry of Moscow and Peking for Communist support in the world would necessarily work in the
direction of more liberal, more democratic, and more
peaceful practices. Among other things, each of the rival-
ing parties may feel constrained to show its revolutionary
irreconcilability and toughness. It is enough to bear in
mind that the need for some kind of public justification will
necessarily figure among the motives of policy makers in
Moscow and Peking.

Great as the effects of the split are likely to be in the
Communist world, they are likely to affect the West even
more. Under the impression of the disunity between Peking and Moscow the Western sense of danger, or, respec-
tively, of security, Western policies toward the Soviet

Union and China, and the Western alliance system have radically changed.

The Soviets have possibly reaped the greatest benefit. Their "coexistence" slogan has all of a sudden received the stamp of credibility by being furiously attacked within the Communist family. Nothing could have so thoroughly persuaded Western leadership of the supposed sincerity of the Kremlin as did the Chinese charges that Soviet policy constituted a "betrayal of the Revolution," a piece of "revisionism," and a sellout to imperialism. The ideological epithets hurled back and forth have struck the West as a revelation through which one could learn the truth about both Moscow and Peking. Since 1962, more and more responsible statesmen in the West have adopted the position that the Soviets have indeed dropped their hostility to "imperialism," are seeking accommodation in the sense of a "live-and-let-live" attitude, and might even be interested in an alliance with the U. S. A. against China. On this premise, policies in Washington and Paris have swung around to the notion that security is no longer to be found in armed defensive capabilities but rather in the pledged word of the Soviet Union. It has become fashionable to declare the Cold War to be a thing of the past, and to accept an "erosion" of Western alliances as a price the West is willing to pay for a wide variety of disarmament agreements, from the Test Ban Treaty to the Non-Proliferation Pact. The pattern extends to the dismantlement of the remaining prohibitions of East-West trade and the repression of Western domestic anti-Communism.

For all practical intents and purposes, the U. S. A. has proclaimed a significant distinction between "good" and "bad" Communists, the "good" Communists being those who supposedly have "evolved" toward liberalism or

"revisionism," the "bad" ones insisting on Leninist irreconcilability. As a result, the U. S. A. decided to follow
two different policies with regard to Communism, one of
accommodation with the "good" Soviets and one of con-
tainment regarding the "bad" Chinese Communists, with
the result that the war in Vietnam, for instance, could not
officially be justified in terms of the Communist danger,
and thus was widely seen as a purely local conflict between
the United States and North Vietnam, or at most, China.
In intellectual circles the conviction that the Soviet Union
has decidedly embraced "coexistence" has engendered
the corresponding notion that it is the United States from
which stem the warlike tendencies in our era. At the same
time, those who are and were radically inclined, have
tended to find in Chinese Communism an ideological
freshness contrasting sharply with the *déjà vu* quality of
Communism in Russia. Thus the Sino-Soviet split has resulted in a new attractiveness of the Communist world in
the West: the Soviet Union appealing to the Western hope
for an enduring peace, and the Chinese Communists excit-
ing the Western longing for some radical renewal. The
dichotomy does not prevent the respective Western adherents of these positions from working with each other in the
broader framework of Western radicalism, just as it does
not exclude practical cooperation between the Soviet Union and China in such situations as Zanzibar, Cuba, and
Vietnam. The West tends to exaggerate the bitterness of
the Sino-Soviet split and to place its own construction on
the situation, instead of observing and analyzing it. It assumes that something which according to this construction should not be does in reality not occur, which is the
same kind of mistake that underlies our construction of

Communist ideology and the conclusion which we too dogmatically infer from it. In fact, the Soviet Union and Communist China not only have cooperated in the midst of their bitter vituperations, but have also utilized the conflict as such in the policies which each of them has followed independently of the other. The Soviet Union, for instance, has been quite content for China to draw on itself the odium of belligerency and irresponsibility from which would accrue to the Soviet Union a reputation of moderation and reasonableness. Under this cover, though, the Soviet Union has pursued most aggressive policies and fomented trouble in many parts of the world; namely, Berlin, Laos, Cuba, Vietnam and, more recently, the Middle East. During this same period China has talked bravely but conducted herself with more than moderation regarding Quemoy and Matsu, her short invasions of India aborting in refusal to engage in a real war, her failure to do anything effective to absorb Macao or Hongkong, at a time when India made short work of Goa. Both the Soviet Union and China have received huge imports from Western countries, on the theory that by helping both of them the West could determine the development of the rift to its own advantage. Potentially the intra-family quarrel among Communists may signal the beginning of the end, an end which in any event would take a long period to move towards its decisive phase; but in the immediate situation the Communists seem to have scored very considerable advances, in terms of diminished Western resistance, divisions within the Western camp, the dissolution of alliances, competition in favor of East-West trade, and effective concealment of Communist cooperation.

CHAPTER 9

Vulnerabilities

of the West

There can be no question that the Soviet "coexistence" slogan has generated an extraordinary response in the West. Particularly since 1962, attitudes and policies stemming from the Cold War premise have been dismantled on a broad front. The process had already begun before the Cuba crisis, with a memorandum of Senator Fulbright of July 11, 1961 (published in the *Congressional Record*, vol. 107, Pt. 11, pp. 14433-39), which led to the so-called "muzzling" of the military, i.e. the prohibition of anti-Communist remarks in speeches by generals and admirals. Later this prohibition was extended to the USIA and other instruments of U.S. propaganda. Anti-Communist intellectuals were attacked by name and officially ostracized. The Supreme Court step by step took down the structure of laws designed to protect this country internally against Communists and their subversive activities. Communists, once banned from most public institutions of learning in this country, began to find wider and wider acceptance as campus speakers and regular faculty members. These measures, in turn, had the effect of persuading large numbers of people that the Communist threat must indeed have passed, so that they operated in the manner of a self-fulfilling prophecy, even though the self-fulfillment occurred wholly on the side of the West, in the public attitudes regarding Communism.

The Pull of the Left

There were many whose views of Communism were not swayed and who began to feel that the sudden lowering of our guard in front of a deadly enemy could stem from nothing but a conspiracy of treason. Most conspiratorial views of history have themselves an ideological character, and this one is no exception. Actually, the receptivity of the West to the Soviet "coexistence" line can be explained readily if one keeps in mind the development of ideas prevalent in leading intellectual circles, ideas that have a certain generic kinship to Communism and thus result in a certain receptivity to Communist appeals. There was such kinship between Nazism and Communism, and both before 1933 and after the end of World War II, Nazis found it quite easy to become Communists, as well as vice versa (the latter, of course, only before the Nazi defeat). From time to time it is necessary to remember that Communism is a growth of the West. There are other ideologies where the Communist one grew, and all these ideologies resemble each other in structure. They all partake in a basic mood of discontent with life and the world which expresses itself in a total critique of all of present-day society, i.e. of every vestige of order and authority known to the present generation. There is the vision of a totally different life, a life free from shortcomings, from evil, from restrictions of all kinds, and all of it realized through some kind of social engineering. There is finally an ethic that is cast in terms of a social cause, in the sense that being or doing good means being against someone or something, and fighting for a certain institutional rearrangement which in turn is considered the culmination of history, the epitome of progress. The fact that Communism, a Western ideology, took organizational, militant shape in the East and picked up some of the qualities of Russian culture, should not cause us to forget that it is in the West that the soil is fertile for all kinds of ideologies and many of them survive in the places where Communism originated. The modicum of inner affinity between them does not mean that they are all compatible with each other; in fact they tend to fly in each other's faces both intellectually and practically.

A basic discontent with the world and total rejection of society and the traditional order have resulted from the work of a number of powerful thinkers: Nietzsche, Auguste Comte, and more recently, Freud and Sartre. The *déraciné*, the intellectual without roots and orientation, has been a familiar figure in the West from France to Russia, since the second half of the 19th century. Since World War II, an existentialist premise that absurdity is the setting of human life has become a widespread fad. Change has been hailed, not for the good it would bring but rather for the destruction it would wreak on all existing order. Religion, church, country, law, morality, and mores alike are being negated in the name of individual "authenticity" and a formless notion of liberty. There are many varieties of this mood, as there are all kinds of ideological justifications for it. Already in the 19th century there arose the slogan for the corresponding kind of conduct: *"épater le bourgeois!"*—shock those who live by the traditional order! That mentality has proved to be most inventive in our days. Deliberate obscenity is used to shock the sense of propriety, deliberate crime to violate the sense of decency, deliberate treason to defy patriotic loyalty, deliberate slovenliness to belittle cleanliness, deliberate ugliness to outrage the sense of beauty. Everywhere a will to pervert wrong into right, low into high, disvalue into value is at work; everywhere not only the symbols but also the contents of the good, the true, and the beautiful are systematically torn down.

It is not an awareness of a higher good, or truth, or beauty that guides these people but rather their premise that there is no order, that the universe is an absurdity, that in a setting of senseless powers and forces man is individually alone, a stranger who at most can achieve a little island of meaning for himself, and maybe his girl friend. This is basically an anarchist outlook. On the other hand, though, the same basic feeling that neither nature nor history has any meaning or order engenders a strong propensity to rely on power. "A world degraded to a power system can only be overcome by power ... countering of power with power is the sole relation to the totality of nature left for man ...," writes Hans Jonas (*The Gnostic Religion*, 2nd ed., 1963, pp. 329 f.). Again, a number of intellectual streams feed this Western awe of power: positivism, nihilism, historicism, scientism. On the one hand, modern man considers himself the Prometheus who, independent of the gods, can make and remake the world according to his own image. On the other hand, the world seen as a conglomeration of soulless and meaningless forces leaves power as the last ground of safety. Moreover, power is considered the most factual of facts, and therefore the most real of realities. A system that develops great power will therefore sooner or later attract many Western intellectuals no matter what their initial judgment of it may have been. One could observe this attraction of power in the case of Neville Chamberlain and of Charles Lindbergh, as one can see it again today in the case of Cyrus Eaton and Senator Fulbright. Power strikes some people —too many, in our days—as a reality that carries its own justification and proves its point by success. This attitude must not be understood as a deliberate cynicism but rather as the result of a vacuum left by the destruction of traditional notions of order and reality.

A British leader at the end of the nineteenth century made the famous remark: "We are all socialists now." This did not become true in any practical sense, however, until forty years later, until the initial suspicion of the Soviet Union had worn off, the United States extended recognition to the Soviet government, and at the same time Nazism appeared in alliance with Fascism as a threat to Western civilization and the peace of the world. At that time many Western intellectuals arrived at a judgment of the world situation that took in not only a moral preference for socialism, but also an assessment of the various forces of the world according to the side to which they belonged. This assessment was summarized for many by Thomas Mann (*Order of the Day*, New York, 1942). He distinguished, in the contemporary world, democracy, socialism, nationalism, Fascism. The essence of Fascism, he said, is force; that of democracy is "the idea" expressed as "truth, freedom, and justice." Socialism appeared to him as "an entirely moral impulse," an "impulse of conscience," which means that "it is turned inward," is "peace-loving even to the point of endangering itself." Nationalism, by contrast, is a "thoroughgoing aggressive impulse, directed against the outer world; its concern is not with conscience but with power; not with human achievement but with war." Fascism, he said, consists in the perversion of socialism to the service of national power purposes. At this point Mann's thought takes an interesting turn, when he divides the world between genuine and false socialism. Democracy, he insists, must develop into socialism, quoting with approval the Belgian leader of the II International, Vandervelde, who proclaimed: "What is essentially and actually new in the world is social democracy." Mann concludes that "this vital moral challenge must be extended not only to the inner structure of the state, but also to the community of states and their international relations," and makes clear his meaning when he mentions "the socialization of raw materials" and a "socially collective system" which would result in a "flourishing world trade."

The crux of these ideas, however, consists in Mann's judgment of Soviet Russia, which deserves to be quoted in full:

"One may wholly disapprove of the example which it sets for internal politics and fear this example. But it must be admitted that the moral nature of all real socialism is substantiated even in the case of Russia; one must recognize it as a peacefully disposed nation. . . . I have perhaps an insufficient awareness of the menace emanating from Russia towards the capitalist social order, for I am no

capitalist. But at least I can see that Russia does not imperil
the essential upon which all else depends—namely, peace
. . . If the world cannot achieve peace and progress, it is
the fault of fascism and not socialism [*Ibid.*, pp. 136 f.].

In other words, Russia's proper place is by the side of
the democracies, the proper future for the democracies is
socialism, peace and socialism sum up the moral intent of
all decent people and determine their confrontation with
Fascism which alone is the repository of brutal force, aggression, and lust for power. These ideas take shape on the
basis of Mann's conviction that the "absolute that has been
given to man" is not identical with Christianity, but rather
with a "new, a third humanism," which will not exhaust
itself in the spirituality of the Christian faith but rather
have "stout-hearted knowledge of man's dark, daemonic,
radically 'natural' side, united with reverence for his super-
biological spiritual worth . . ." (p. 164). The cause of this
"humanism" demands the alignment of Russia with the
West: "It is upon the contact between the two and their
mutual adjustment that the hope of the world depends—
the social reform and rejuvenation of western democracy,
and the humanization of eastern collectivism."
    Here is the same mentality that at present acclaims
loudly the progressing "coexistence" with Soviet Russia.
Democracy and Soviet Russia are akin in their common
devotion to peace and socialism; they will and must approach each other in their social and political development; while certain features of the Soviet regime deserve
disapproval and may even constitute a danger to our social
order, that does not detract from the basic moral goodness
of Communism. This appraisal of the world's political
forces has become the perennial, frequently silent, premise

of large parts of the Western intelligentsia on both sides of the Atlantic, as well as of those leaders in other countries who, as Nehru, have been formed in Western schools. In practice, this means that they cannot conceive of real hostility involving movements of the Left: *"pas d'ennemi à gauche!"* In other words, the essential enemy can be only on the Right, the Right being designated in terms of Fascism and Nazism even though it may include many individuals and forces who do not fit into this categorization. Where there is blame for political disasters, it is made to fall on the Right while the Left is absolved; when one is neutral, one's neutrality is conceived as favoring the Left but opposing the Right; when rights are demanded, they are meant exclusively for the Left but never for the Right; when hopes are voiced, they look only to the Left and never to the Right.

Banning Anti-Communism

This pattern appeared to be workable so long as the Right consisted of Hitler and Mussolini. After their defeat, however, the pattern continued, and now there is a tendency to make these same distinctions with Soviet Russia as the Left and the United States as the Right, the latter being defined as "Right" by virtue of being locked in a struggle with the Soviet Union, which is of course identified as "the Left." One can summarize these attitudes as follows: a) The West is not essentially endangered by Communism, but only by its own social imperfections and atomic war; b) Anti-Communism is reactionary and potentially Fascist; c) International tensions are mainly the fault of "cold warriors" and militarists in the West and could be

made to disappear if we changed our "aggressive" policies;
d) The time has come for a "dialogue" and the building of
a working community with the Soviets.

Now it is a fact that the Communist ideology, laid down
in the writings of Lenin, Marx, Engels, Stalin, Khrushchev, Brezhnev, and Kosygin, centers on the principle of
an essential and irreconcilable hostility of Communists
toward everything that is of the West, precisely toward the
liberal, democratic, peace-hoping and peace-preaching
bourgeois civilization which the Communists consider the
chief obstacle to the realization of their future society. For
this reason those who maintain the above-mentioned attitudes must assert that the ideology does not represent
Communism, either because it is alleged always to have
been an afterthought, or because it has gradually given
way to other modes of thought and reasons for action. This
allegation takes on different forms. Some like to say that
underlying Communism is the Russian mentality, that the
Communists are difficult because, and only because, the
Russians always have been difficult. Others see in Communism nothing but traditional Russian nationalism, and
nothing in Communist policies but the interests of a great
power preoccupied with problems of its national security.
Still others speak of a mysterious "law" of history called
the "loss of revolutionary élan," which, if one looks
closely, is derived from only one example, the French
Revolution, and even there cannot be supported by the
facts. Still others postulate an inevitable "convergence" of
the Communist regime and our society, implicitly assuming that it is differences of social systems that originally
caused the conflict. They expose themselves to the scornful rejoinder of a Soviet writer in *International Affairs*: "In

other words, there is neither capitalism nor socialism: there are only variations on the theme of a single industrial society. This theory is patently wrong, for it simply disregards the facts." Similarly, the Russian writer Andrei Amalric dismisses the hope that the Soviet regime will become more similar to Western systems as naive: "We may get socialism with bare knees, but certainly not with a human face." Since the optimistic views of Soviet evolution stem from either wishful thinking or the overshadowing fear of an atomic conflict, they are not subject to the usual discipline of discussion. Someone who, in keeping with the evidence, maintains that the ideology has always been central to the phenomenon of Communism is treated as if he were speaking from sinister motives, as one whose arguments reveal a "Fascist mentality," or a tendency toward "warmongering." For it is alleged that if one were to assume that Communism is rooted in an irrational ideology, the conclusion of an atomic showdown would inevitably follow. Such a conclusion, however, follows neither in logic nor in political reality. Rather, it emerges from the above-mentioned simplistic polarization of political forces in the world, by virtue of which the Communists are defined as peace-loving and everyone opposed to them as preferring war and oppressive power. The entire argument recalls Adlai Stevenson's delightful quip: "On these conclusions will I base my facts."

The same polarization of forces dictates the judgments by which the United States is one-sidedly blamed for the world's present tensions. If Cuba fell to Communism, it was because our allegedly unfriendly attitude had "forced" Castro to throw himself into Moscow's arms. Any trouble in Latin America can only be interpreted as the result of

this country's failure to back the various revolutionary
movements south of the Rio Grande. Tension over Berlin?
It stems from the stubbornness of the United States in
clinging to an outmoded and untenable agreement; or,
alternatively, from our failure to "neutralize" Germany.
The war in Vietnam is a case of United States aggression;
our deployment of troops in areas threatened by Communists must be attributed to the Pentagon's militarism. The
fact of our possession of atomic weapons in itself is im-
moral, and thus any future possibility of nuclear war must
be put on the debit account of America. One professor of
political science wrote a book "proving" that the Cold War
must be laid entirely at the door of the United States.
Finally, this attitude turns from such accusations to revolutionary intentions: American society must be changed,
so that no nuclear war will occur. In this extreme form, of
course, such views are held only by a relatively small group
of people. The pattern has many shadings, though, and in
its most widely spread form turns up as a "moral symmetry" that opposes to every evil of Communism a corresponding one of our society. The whole picture then
becomes a contest between two entities of similar quality
and nature, namely two societies, each having its own
preferred features and being accused of them by the other,
with some of the accusations founded, others not, but the
whole being essentially a tit-for-tat making no sense.

Enduring Peace: Ideology of the West

A third ideological *idée fixe* that renders the West vul-
nerable to the present Communist offensive is the vision
of enduring peace. Communism has rightly been called a

kind of millennium, a mythical vision of complete this-worldly harmony and bliss. In this sense, enduring peace is the millennium of the West, particularly of the Anglo-Saxon countries. It must, of course, not be confused with the concept of peace as the termination and/or avoidance of war, which is no *idée fixe* and belongs to no particular age or culture. Enduring peace is rather the vision of the institutionalized banning of war from a world in which nations continue to exist with their own governments, with no higher authority to which they are responsible, and with their own systems of maintaining law and order. It is, of course, this condition which has made war possible in the past, and which admits of no guarantee that war will not occur in the future. Each nation by itself can be called an institution of peace, in that the maintenance of armed force is monopolized by the government, which enforces law, punishes violators, and breaks up disturbances of the public order. Not even such institutions can guarantee the perpetuity of harmony and prevent such calamities as civil wars; still, they provide sufficient assurance of peace for people to go about their business unarmed and unworried, at least in most cases. After World War I, Woodrow Wilson made himself the champion of the Western millennium of enduring peace, the same year in which Lenin appeared on the world scene as the champion of the Communist millennium. Wilson's legacy was the League of Nations, from which in turn the United Nations derived. The idea was to provide a machinery for the peaceful settlement of disputes between nations. It would be effective only if all nations trusted it so implicitly that they acquired the habit of submitting to it all their differences, which would then be composed without resort to violence.

It was clear from the beginning that the scheme could not contain an enforcement machinery; nations were too powerful to be forced, and force would only lead to more war, which was precisely what was to be excluded. Thus the basis of universal adherence to the scheme would be *confidence*. Nations must gain confidence, first of all, that abiding by the scheme would not be to their disadvantage; secondly, that other nations would abide by the scheme too. One could not expect this confidence to be there at the beginning, so the theory went on to argue, since international politics was still beset with the mutual suspicions that have bred wars. But any gain in confidence would serve to create its own momentum toward enduring peace. Gradually increasing confidence, indeed, is the only road to the realization of the vision. This is not the place to go into that part of the peace ideology which deals with the —supposedly isolated and rare—cases of aggression and how to cope with them. Suffice it to say that not collective action against aggression but rather increasing confidence in peaceful ways of settling disputes was meant to be the crux of institutionalized world peace.

The peace millennium has a certain kinship with the Communist ideology, because it too envisages a world in which human existence has been permanently transformed and liberated from the burden of its own imperfections. What is more, it believes that this goal can be attained by human efforts. The efforts in the case of enduring peace, however, lie mainly in the realm of psychology, since the full realization of the millennium hinges on a psychological transformation: the shedding of old fears and suspicions, the adoption of confidence in certain procedures, and confidence of one nation in another.

When the League of Nations fell considerably short of expectations, when disarmament faltered, when, finally, in Germany an extremist movement gained power on the strength of anti-Versailles emotions, the chief advocates of the peace millennium, particularly the British, did not revert to the usual precautions of power politics as, for instance, armaments and alliances, but rather tried to cope with the explosive situation through the psychology of "increasing confidence." The results contributed to the further deterioration of the situation and thus to the coming of World War II. The example of the Thirties is mentioned here only in order to show that the enduring peace ideology had practical consequences in Western policies even before the Communist threat became acute.

The invention of nuclear weapons and the prospect of a war of unacceptable devastation lent special urgency to these millenarian expectations. Against this background, not only the Soviet proclamation of "peaceful coexistence" but, particularly, also the implementation of this line in Khrushchev's withdrawal of missiles from Cuba was accepted at face value. Here it is important to remember that one of the elements in the Western millennium of enduring peace is the postulate of a "civilized state," i.e. a state that has left behind the atavism of belligerent moods and tastes and has grown to the maturity of peaceful settlement. The League of Nations was built on the assumption that after the defeat of the Kaiser no modern nation could still be called uncivilized in that respect, and that lapses into warlike atavism would be wholly accidental and could easily be corrected by concerted pressures. In spite of Thomas Mann's definitions, the conduct of the Soviet Union after World War II, particularly at Berlin and in Greece and Korea, raised grave doubts about the maturity of that government. It was in this atmosphere of genuine concern about Soviet rationality that the ideological explanation of Communism found wide acceptance in the West. From 1956 on, however, and even as early as the Korean settlement, many of the West's leaders began to feel that Russia, after all, was becoming civilized. If that were true, then the efforts to build peace on mutual and common confidence could be resumed, since they might now lead to the millennium of world peace. At this point, then, the method of "gradually increasing confidence" began to dominate Western, and particularly American, policy making. The goal of disarmament involved the banning and abolition of nuclear weapons. The West insisted on inspection and international control which were and are unacceptable to the Soviet Union. On the theory that the appetite would grow as one began to eat, a partial problem was then tackled: atomic testing. When inspection and control turned out to be the stumbling block even in this limited affair, the West dropped the requirement. The supposed gain: increased confidence. In other words, the intangible factor of mutual confidence has become a real policy objective for which the West is willing to trade tangibles of considerable importance. This approach was tried once before, in the matter of international regulation of commodities and reduction of tariffs. At the end of the Twenties, governments saw with concern how their fearful nationalism in economic policies was pushing the world deeper and deeper into a depression. All attempts to tackle the situation on a broad scale failed. It was finally decided that if governments could agree on the international handling of one particular item, their success would then make possible further advances so that the bigger problem would eventually yield to a step-by-step advance or order. The item selected was hides. An international convention on skins and hides was agreed upon, but that was all. No further agreements flowed from this one, and the theory of the increasing momentum of confidence was not borne out by the facts. In the Sixties, all the same, this theory was reapplied. The Test Ban Treaty was concluded, not as an end in itself, but explicitly as the stepping stone to further agreements, which rationale seemed to justify the renunciation of its demand for inspection by the West. The same thinking applied to the American government's wheat sale to the Soviet Union on which we dropped the requirement of cash payment and agreed to long-term credit. The Non-Proliferation Treaty is a further case in point. That treaty would make sense only if its scope were universal and enforceable, leaving aside the question of whether one could trust the present group of nuclear powers with enforcement. On the theory of increasing confidence, however, the West was disposed to settle for part of a loaf, even if that should work out to its own disadvantage and the disadvantage of its allies.

Modern diplomacy has always counted with intangibles; in other words, it bases its calculations not only on the capabilities but also on the intents of governments. The memoirs of famous diplomats are full of accounts of how these men arrived at their insights into another government's motives and inhibitions. In so far as Western thinking and practice are based, however, on the peace ideology, we have abandoned the cautious and concretely evaluating approach of shrewd diplomacy. In its place we have substituted a general belief, independent of all experience, in the necessary and gradual growth of "civilized attitudes" in governments and particularly of that elusive "confidence" which is supposed to heal all shortcomings of international politics. At present, United States policy has come to rely on this factor to an extent which later historians will find hard to believe. In an article in *Foreign Affairs* in 1965, America's then "duke of disarmament," William C. Foster, declared that an "erosion of alliances" would have to be accepted for the sake of Soviet-American cooperation, i. e. for a gain in "mutual confidence." Underlying this trade of tangible elements of strength for intangible and ultimately wishful psychological gains is a theory that through such assumed increases in mutual confidence the Soviet government will be "educated," that it will turn out in the end to be less Communist, less atavistic, and will then become a good and useful citizen of the world. Every ideology implies the enormous arrogance of a movement that believes itself capable, by "correct" strategy, of out-flanking the ancient evils of human existence and then totally conquering them. The ideology of millenarian peace is no exception. It proceeds in terms of a Second Reality which is not yet here and has no foundation in historical reality, which dictates policies that are unsuited to situations as they are, and thus causes a deterioration of such international stability as we have been able to enjoy thus far.

The End of Monolithic Communism

A final vulnerability of the West stems from the frequently heard argument that Communism is "no longer a monolith," that, being divided, it has ceased to be a threat or, to go even further, that there is no longer any such thing as "Communism." The division of world Communism is certainly a fact; we have traced some of the vain attempts to restore unity in Communist ranks. The days of the Comintern are gone forever; even the Cominform with its mainly East European compass can no longer be called a working reality. There is still the Warsaw Pact, to be sure, but few would be so rash as to claim that the Soviet Union could reliably count on the armies of Czechoslovakia, Hungary, and Poland. In the West, this uncertainty is more than matched by the de jure defection of France from NATO and the destruction of military communication lines traversing that country. All the same, let us now assume that Communist regimes have no purpose in common any more, that they operate politically and militarily apart from each other, and that we are facing a plurality of Communisms with a variety of strategies and goals. There still remain a number of developments in the field of international power, each of which is bound to have ultimate significance in terms of human lives and the order of freedom.

First, there is Southeast Asia, centering in the war in Vietnam. Sir Robert Thompson, a British observer strongly critical of the American conduct of the war, has nevertheless emphasized that, were South Vietnam to fall to the Communists (be they described as Vietcong, National Liberation Front, or North Vietnamese), the rest of Southeast Asia would follow like a set of dominoes. Being aware of the resistance to the domino theory in the United States, he based his conclusions on what the "dominoes" themselves say. He might also have pointed to the stark military facts: North Vietnam has invaded South Vietnam with a force of seven divisions, not to speak of replacements of casualties; it has invaded Laos with a force of over 50,000 men, Cambodia with more than 40,000 regular troops, and is invading Thailand with an increasing number of agents who organize the hill tribes for guerilla warfare and promote general insurgency in the entire countryside. The pivot of all these efforts is South Vietnam. Once the Communists are no longer interdicted there, no non-Communist regime from Rangoon to Manila can still feel safe. The results of such a Communist triumph would not be confined to what one might call "national independence." In Hué, during the Tet-Offensive, the Communists massacred more than 3,000 civilians, first murdering "selected victims" in order to strike terror in the rest, and then, when they believed they had definitely conquered the city, liquidating the "social negatives," i.e., all those who might be deemed to stand in their way. Finally, when they had to evacuate, they systematically killed all the witnesses to their murders and anyone who might identify the Vietcong cadres who, during the offensive, had emerged from hiding and thus made their true identity known. This pattern would obviously obtain for all of the future invasions. Would it make any difference whether the victorious Communists were natives, adherents of Peking, or Moscow, or even of Tito? Would it matter whether their weapons were forged in China, or Czechoslovakia, or Cuba? Would the Laotians have a better fate to look forward to if Peking and Moscow were at each other's throats? or in each other's arms? Would the area be more irretrievably lost to freedom if Communism still enjoyed worldwide unity?

Another area of acute conflict is the Middle East. Whatever one may think about the merits of the dispute between Israel and the Arabs, there can be no question that the open tension with the threat of war stems from the massive delivery of Soviet arms to Egypt and its allies, first in 1956, then again after the short but clear-cut military victory of Israel in 1967. At the same time, the Soviet Union has exercised a certain restraint on Nasser, which has given rise to U. S. hopes for a concerted Soviet-American policy to pacify the area. One wonders, though, whether a settlement between Israel and the Arabs is really a Soviet objective. After all, Israel is the condition that causes Nasser's dependence on the Soviet Union, induces him to open naval bases to the Soviet fleet, to admit Soviet military personnel to his air force and Soviet technicians to his economy. Egypt, Syria, and Iraq are the three Arab countries in the area officially committed to a flamboyant, socialist Leftism, with Communists enjoying considerable permissiveness in the last two. The real issue in the Middle East does not seem to be Israel, but the eventual inclusion of Jordan, Saudi Arabia, Kuwait, and Yemen in an all-over socialist bloc that can be infiltrated at will by Soviet agents and that looks to the Soviet Union as its deliverer. Such a bloc would flank not only Turkey but also Africa and, with the help of Algeria and Libya, the Mediterranean. If this development were to be consummated, what difference would it make whether there were Chinese and Soviet versions of Communism? The effects of such a power bloc would be all against freedom and all in favor of Communist inhumanity.

A third area to be watched consists of Italy and France, the former having fallen into a political and social crisis that seems to be terminal in some way, and the latter

depending for stability only on a residual Gaullist movement without de Gaulle. Much was made of the independence of Italian Communists at the June 1969 Moscow
conference, of their propensity to adapt Communism to
Italian conditions, their willingness to wield power without dictatorship. "Italian Communism will be unlike Russian Communism," so goes the comforting thought that is
to reconcile us to future developments in that country. The
argument is frequently based on the motives of the masses
who vote Communist in elections, or on the psychology of
the rank-and-file members of the Communist Party who
seem more Italian or even Catholic than Communist, according to Guareschi's delightful novels. What the Communist Party would do when it got hold of a part or the
whole of governmental power in Italy, however, would be
decided not by the masses or the cadres but by a few Party
leaders who would use the support that is theirs as they
saw fit. Now it is entirely possible that they would see fit
to conduct themselves as if the Communist Party of Italy
were just another Western political party playing the political game according to the traditional rules of democracy.
If they did, however, their decision would probably be
motivated by the consideration that if Communists in
power in Italy behaved respectably and reasonably, Communists in France would have a much improved chance of
entering the government either as coalition partners or as
the ruling party. A Communist-controlled Italy without
France would be something gained but would in the long
run hardly be considered a defensible position. Italy with
France, however, would mean a Communist Europe. In
the long run, again, a Communist regime in Italy and
France would not leave the country intact, as would a

regime of democratic socialists. It would subvert not only the political system but also economics and culture, particularly religion. If a party calling itself Communist refrained from something amounting to total subversion in Italy or France, another more radical party would immediately form to the left and push for the radical revolution that "would not even leave the pillars of the house standing." In any event, either Italy or France under Communist-controlling influence would be lost to the West for political or military purposes, and by the same token would be open to Soviet political and military operations. Again, it makes little difference whether the Italian Communists "adapt Communism to Italian conditions." An Italian Communism is likely to differ from Russian Communism in any event, just as Communism in China differed from Russian Communism. To Italians, deprived of everything they call their own, not merely property but religion, morality, law, church, school, customs, and tradition, it would matter little whether the operation was performed Italian, or Russian, or Chinese style.

Finally, Cuba. We hear a great deal about the *sui generis* character of Castro's revolution and the superficiality and artificiality of his adherence to Marxism-Leninism. The implication of this argument generally is to point out an advantage for the West. Cuba does not conform wholly to the Soviet model, *ergo* it must be better. At a time when many people with radical Leftist inclinations show a certain amount of fed-upness with Soviet Communism, however, Castro's difference may be a decided asset for the other side. There can be no question about the appeal of Castro in Latin America. It is Castro who actively promotes violence and revolution throughout the region, in opposition to Soviet-controlled, official Communist parties. Castro, however, is able to do this only by virtue of financial subsidies and arms deliveries from the Soviet Union. If he is successful in setting up his men in control over a Latin American country, will the people of that country be better off because Castro has not been an orthodox Communist? Will their country be less open to Soviet infiltration and power use than if Castro had been trained in Moscow? Will this country display less hostility to the United States than one made Communist through Soviet occupation troops?

Communist power, under whatever auspices it may be established, is invariably hostile to human nature, to freedom, and to the countries that still resist Communism with all their might. The Rumanian government may have maneuvered itself into something like a little independence from Moscow, but its rule over its subject-victims is as hard as that of Moscow itself. It may trade with the West, but its troops and warships go into maneuvers with the Soviet army and navy. In the arena of international politics, the power contests may look complex and, indeed, polycentric. The issue, however, is simple and everywhere the same: will people fall under a regime that is determined to deprive them of their beliefs, values, traditions, and allegiances and turn them into cogs of a production machine, or will they not? What happens to people under a Communist regime is always and everywhere basically the same; what happens to them outside the Communist world is a matter of many variegated possibilities. It is in neither our power nor our intention to bestow on the entire non-Communist world democratic institutions. Those outside the Iron and Bamboo Curtains may indeed live in democracies, or under generals' juntas, in absolute monarchies, or under civilian autocrats, in one-party oligarchies, or on the brink of political chaos. We are not responsible for establishing good government all over the world. We are, however, the only power with sufficient strength to counter the atom bomb–supported Communist threat to non-Communist nations, and this capability to deny the Communists their will and design on others is our negative but very solemn mission in this time and age.

CHAPTER 10

The End of Communism?

The problem of change has moved into the center of our policy decisions regarding Communism. Great changes have been observed within the last decade: de-Stalinization, the "peaceful coexistence" policy, the Sino-Soviet rift, the loosening up of the Soviet bloc, the introduction of the so-called Liberman reforms. What do these happenings portend? Are they to be understood as parts of a movement in Russia toward an ordinary regime with peaceful aspirations? Is Communism being replaced by some other guiding principle, and if so, could this be a principle of toleration and cooperation, of welfare and liberty, or even justice? Do these changes manifest the existence of forces operating in Russian society which the Communist rulers are powerless to resist, or psychological processes by which the mind of revolutionaries mellows toward some kind of philistine short-range self-interest? It is a measure of the intellectual flabbiness of the West that these questions are in general being answered wishfully, sentimentally, superficially, and uncritically. Even where something like scientific method is brought to bear upon them, it frequently serves more to justify preconceived conclusions than to discipline the mind. Much of this failing must be attributed to poverty of imagination in grasping the reality of totalitarianism, which differs so radically from any normal society. Intellectuals too frequently tend to project the assumptions of our own world into the Communist regime.

Total State, No Society

One of these assumptions is the distinction between state and society that has played such a large and important role in Western social sciences. The state, as the machinery of deliberate and purposeful political action, is set off against the background of society, the pattern of interacting individual and group activities, institutions, customs, other than the state. The concept has been used to explore factors which condition government; for instance, through what is called "group theory," focusing on the clusters of relations and activities, loyalties and hierarchies which reflect typical aspirations of individual people. A group of spontaneously coalescing individuals is a pattern worth studying, but there are patterns other than groups, and thus other social scientists devote their attention to patterns of voting, judicial decisions, buying, schooling, and so on. Projected into the future, these patterns appear as trends. Price trends, for instance, presuppose a pattern of prices which can be observed to follow something like its own laws. Even the layman uses the notion of a price pattern, for instance, to inform himself about a foreign country as he finds out the prices of certain

key commodities and then draws conclusions regarding
the rest of the prices. As such nonpolitical structures and
regularities are observed and studied, we assume that besides the power of government there are other centers of
power in society, for instance in business, trade unions,
consumer groups, religious, and other groups. We seek to
understand politics by reducing political changes to
changes in the structures and orientations of society.

This approach, valid for any country in which the forces
of society are allowed even a modicum of leeway, is not
suitable for the understanding of totalitarian regimes.
Western intellectuals are inclined to take the existence of
a "society" as distinct from the "state" for granted, and we
are no longer aware that "society" presupposes a mode of
human existence in which the order of procuring a livelihood is separate from that of law, police, and public peace.
In totalitarian countries, however, the government combines in its hands all of these functions. It is lawmaker as
well as employer, police as well as producer, judge as well
as distributor of goods, commander of military forces as
well as banker. There is no private sector, and thus no
economic and existential foundation that would enable
people to form a social force varying from that of the
government, or even maintain indifference toward public
policy. In a totalitarian system, opposition is tantamount
to renunciation of one's livelihood, and to differ with the
government means to opt for chaos. Totalitarianism means
that the state has completely absorbed society. No centers
or bases of power are permitted to exist apart from the
government or to arise from the spontaneous choices of
individuals. Every organization is a government, or rather,
a party organization, every institution is a public institu-

tion, every relationship is a party-controlled relationship, and every position of authority is a party-sanctioned authority. Human existence is dominated by a monopoly of power, organization, and initiative, beside which no other powers, organizations, or initiatives are tolerated.

The absorption of society into the state goes so far that one must be extremely cautious when speaking of "groups" in a totalitarian regime. To us a group is something manifesting spontaneous choices and inclinations. In Communist totalitarianism, groups are almost exclusively instigated by public officials. Every sports club, chess club, literary club has been formed by the government. Previously existing groups have been either dissolved or else taken under firm control, often by means of infiltration. The family is no longer an inward-turned group; the children now carry official indoctrination into it and inside information out to the officials. Nor does it make much sense to talk of classes in a regime where nobody belongs to a certain class on the grounds of birth, property, education, or culture, but everybody is where he is because he has been put there by the rulers. Much is being made of a supposedly rising Soviet "bourgeoisie" or "middle class." In the West, distinct characteristics are associated with the term "middle class," by which we habitually connote a class of proprietors whose strength consisted of their economic independence based on private property which no government dared to touch. Its relative independence from higher-ups, both its social betters and the political rulers, was guaranteed by a system of law based on an independent judiciary and raised to a modicum of security above and beyond political will. In a totalitarian regime law is not inviolate, property provides no political inde-

pendence, individuals or classes of individuals have no
strength over against the rulers. The Party has used the
government machinery to spot and hunt out all the elements from which groups or individuals derived a certain
amount of personal security, to destroy them, and to replace them with ties of helpless dependence on officialdom. Soviet Communism acknowledges only one residue
of what we call "society": that which Lenin identified as
the "terrible force of habit," a power which he feared and
yet could not vanquish by a frontal attack. The totalitarian
mind is characterized by its declaration of war on this last
vestige of spontaneous social order. No trace of "society"
can be tolerated, rather every bit of structure must stem
from deliberate official decisions and be maintained by
official control. Thus concepts based on the Western distinction of "state" and "society" are unsuitable for an
understanding of this regime. Group theories and trend
studies are misplaced in this context. The understanding
of a totalitarian regime is a matter of extreme difficulty for
which one must create new concepts and research tools.
This is not the place to develop such concepts, but a few
hints may be in order.

In the first place, we must rid our mind of the habit of
assuming something like natural laws behind every relationship, pattern, or trend. Whatever occurs in this
totalitarian regime must be reduced to some bureaucratic
will, even though one must distinguish between the original bureaucratic intent and the eventual social or political
result. A suitable concept might be *the will of the pasha*.
When Turkish officialdom ruled alien subject peoples,
these subjects had to depend on their ability to guess the
will of their *pasha*, the bureaucrat whose every whim was

law. No shared principle, no constitution, no objective law, no administrative tradition provided any clue to what the *pasha* would do to them and about them. Totalitarianism sets up its rule on a rejection of all limitations of public power stemming from morality, religion, constitution, law, or tradition. All the same, there is a difference. The *pasha* or modern totalitarian is himself controlled and governed by a collective fancy, his Party's ideology. Thus something is known about his will. It is a collective will, the will of the Party. The subjects of this totalitarian can know this much: the *pasha* considers himself a part of an enterprise that is at war with what people normally are and traditionally have been; he wants to remake them in his ideological image: he wants their support in the form of hard work, a kind of universal *corvée*; all benefits which he distributes are means to obtain these ends of his. In a totalitarian regime, the *will of the pasha* is experienced as an alien power even where no nationality problem deepens the rift. In a sense the burden of the regime is easier where Communist rule appears to the people in the form of an alien nationality, because the foreignness of the ruler there is attributed to nationality rather than ideology.

The subjects of totalitarianism confront the *pasha* not only as a ruling collective but also as the local bureaucrat. One might be tempted to say that knowledge of the ways of a totalitarian bureaucracy is the equivalent of the knowledge of "society" in nontotalitarian systems. In his relation to the subjects, the local *pasha* is not limited by law, religion, morality, or tradition, but he does labor under the limitation of the will of his central *pasha*. That will is to him also an alien power because it is not understood on the ground of shared principles and concepts. The local *pasha* often acts unpredictably because the Party line, although representing an ideology espoused by all Party members, frequently takes inscrutable turns and thus confronts the lower ranks with the demand of unconditional and uncomprehending submission. The local *pasha* is thus governed by fear of the higher *pasha*, and the demands of this fear are not calculable; not to him and not to his subjects. From this fear, for instance, flows the ubiquitous disposition of all minor bureaucrats constantly to lie, to put up major and minor Potemkin villages daily and hourly. Since they are never sure of their guesses as to what precisely is expected of them, they tend to hedge, simulate, conceal, and camouflage. Eyewitness reports as well as Soviet news sources are full of examples of irrational official conduct, actions that cannot simply be explained in terms of the bigness of organization but well up from the self-willed alienation of Communist leadership from the underlying people and from the rank and file of their own Party. All the same, bureaucratic initiative and direction are the key to everything that happens in the Soviet regime, and if one would reduce patterns, trends, relationships to their underlying causes, one should follow the maxim: *cherchez le pasha.*

Liberalization?

It is one thing to say that Soviet totalitarianism has a single power center and thus knows of only two classes: the rulers and the ruled, and quite another to claim for that power center an unlimited ability to have its will. Power deals with people who are not like bricks, and relations and social processes have subtleties that may thwart the designs of even the most total power. Particularly, ideologically oriented power is bound to run up against realities which it has resolved to ignore. The question then is whether such circumstances can impose changes on the design of the rulers as well as on their monopolistic position. To be concrete: de-Stalinization has its own momentum from which stem certain difficulties for the Communist Party. For what it is worth, de-Stalinity has become some kind of political legitimacy in Sovietland. Someone causing suspicion that he might restore Stalinist terror methods would be politically shunned. Thus there are certain things which a rising Party politician may not do. Does this force Communists to adopt democracy as their guiding principle? If we compare the rule of the Communist Party with the absolute monarchy in Western Europe, from about 1500 to about 1800, we find that absolute kings also confronted a number of religious, political, legal, and economic obstacles to their will but all the same did not change the concept of their rule and the intent of absolutism until their overthrow by insurrections if at all. The continuity in Communist rule is far more intense than in the monarchy, for the Party continues by co-optation, i.e. by drawing to itself men of its own spirit. Thus de-Stalinization must be understood as an external rather than an internal inhibition, an obstacle rather than a change of heart.

The same is true in economics. The problems in the Soviet economy stem from the Party's own activities. Such problems have arisen periodically, in 1920, 1924–6, and again in the Thirties. The so-called Liberman reforms constitute an attempt to deal with the problems of cost accounting and plant efficiency which had not yielded to many other attempted efforts at solution. Even though the technique of marketing is borrowed from capitalism, one cannot assume an intention of the Party to convert the Soviet economy into a market-type economy with a centrally uncontrolled movement of prices and unplanned pattern of micro-economic decisions. Even though a particular plant is permitted to make and use profits, no class of profit-minded individuals is likely to result from it, for the plant manager owes his position not to his earnings and savings but only to Party-controlled appointment and can be dropped into the ranks of common labor by a stroke of the pen, of which personal insecurity he is continuously aware. What is more, the Communist Party in its history has shown repeated inclination to subordinate economic to political considerations. In dealing with certain economic problems along what people in the West consider unorthodox lines, the Party intends not to undermine its political power but to enhance it.

What is one to think of the following kind of incident? At Moscow University a routine student meeting conducted by a Party agitprop man turned into a free-for-all heckling session in which the students expressed more and more boldly their skepticism with regard to the socialist life. They claimed they had never seen it and wanted to know what it is like. The Party agent found himself on the defensive and eventually retreated in confusion. Is this an indication that the ideology is waning and has lost its hold on the young generation? That kind of conclusion, widespread in the West, rests on the assumption that the students at some time were true believers in Communism. This assumption is mistaken, not only on observed evidence but also on the Party's own showing. The precedent of Nazi Germany showed that incessant Party indoctrination had never penetrated more than skin-deep and was quickly shaken off by the young generation. The same could be observed in the case of Hungary. The above-mentioned incident thus raises two questions: a) why were the students, who may never have been convinced of the Communist ideology, bolder than ever before in the voicing of their doubts? and b) can we assume that the Party agitprop man had lost his previous Communist convictions? Obviously, there is not a shred of evidence for the latter thesis because a hostile audience is nothing new to Communists and does not necessarily reflect on the motivation of those who represent the Party point of view. As for the former, it is clear that de-Stalinization has been taken as a kind of general loosening of the regime by the subjects, who feel emboldened to try out what they consider their newly obtained modicum of liberty. The report failed to inform us whether the students got away with their heckling, but the incident was followed in short order by the trial and condemnation of the two poets, Daniel and Syniawsky, both of whom had also believed that the day of intellectual freedom had dawned. Nor will the Party necessarily be compelled to return to full-fledged Stalinist terror, so long as it can practice a little intimidation here and a little there and maintain a general atmosphere of insecurity.

In a totalitarian regime no change in quality should be expected from compulsions of the society on the Party and the government. Totalitarianism is ideologically at war with the society, and the longer it has wielded power, the less likely it is that any power centers have survived in society that could bring effective pressure to bear on the single power center of Party government. Circumstances indeed may develop, mainly by the Party's own doings, which hem in and confront the Party with bothersome obstacles to its ambitions. Such conditions, however, have always been known to the Party. Moreover, it is practically impossible for any particular group, an "anti-Party" group, to take advantage of such embarrassments of the Party. Whatever compulsions may issue from circumstances will be wholly impersonal and purposeless environmental compulsions, which the Party will seek to overcome by evasion, retreat, or more effective compulsions. All this will not change the pattern of a single center of power, organization, or initiative in a sea of individuals, each of whom is reduced to utter impotence and can find no way of alleviating his helplessness. The salient fact in a totalitarian regime is the total pulverization of what used to be a social fabric. A person no longer finds anything in his relations to others that he can call his own. The realization of his human essence in company with others has come to depend wholly on someone else's initiative, someone else's direction, to which he can do nothing more than lend his support. The salient fact is the exclusive concentration of all social relatedness in Party domination, coupled with the self-willed alienation of the Party from its subjects, an alienation that results from the Communist ideology. Thus, while the circumstances, including human attitudes, with which the Party has to deal may develop in a wide range of possibilities, there is little likelihood that the basic fact of Party monopolization of societal contexts will alter. Nor can one assume that the Party's intent will in time adopt a different character. There are good psychological reasons against such an assumption: Those who rise in the Communist Party are men and women whose ideological reliability has been successfully tested in countless different assignments, committee meetings, and intra-Party quarrels. Once at the top, these people need their ideological beliefs as sources of energy, direction, and courage. They have neither time nor inclination to reexamine their assumptions while operating from day to day. Nor would they feel any particular need to do so. Their ideology postulates certain conditions for the ultimate realization of their vision, and as they look at the contemporary world they need not conclude that developments have moved wholly contrary to their expectations. In this sense, the rise of the Russian living standard would tend to confirm their Communist convictions rather than weaken them, particularly since the Communist ideology in the first place did not stem from primary experiences of poverty but rather from an alleged knowledge of the "laws of history." In a totalitarian regime which has succeeded in organizing a tight-knit unity of the ruling group while scattering all potential rival agglomerations, it does not take a great number to keep millions of helpless individual people subjected to the center's will. The Communist Party has a core of cadres who are heavily indoctrinated, magnificently disciplined, personally committed, and effectively articulate. That core in the Soviet Union numbers approximately half a million people. Through them, tens of millions of lower Party members, Komsomols, Trade Union officials, and government bureaucrats are manipulated. As long as the core of cadres maintains its own unity, as long, in other words, as rival groups within the Party do not openly fall out with each other, each succeeding in arming its own power apparatus, there is no change in circumstances that can affect the nature of this totalitarian regime.

What Evidence of the End?

All the same, since nothing human lasts forever, Communism will one day come to an end. What evidence of its demise can we expect to see? How will we know when Communists can no longer be called Communists? Significant change would affect the basic determination of the Communist cadres. Leaders would appear who no longer base their thinking on the assumption of irreconcilable class struggle. In fact, there already have been such leaders: Kolakowski in Poland, Dubcek in Czechoslovakia, and Djilas and Mihailov in Yugoslavia. It was not a conversion to Christianity or some kind of personal difficulty which caused them to reject Communist ideology, but rather the impulse of socialist thinking itself, so that one can speak here of some kind of Communist evolution. "I do not know what socialism is," said Kolakowski, "but I do know, comrades, that it is a good thing." In other words, some kind of idealistic belief in socialist goodness brought Kolakowski to reject the Communist regime and its concept of protracted struggle. Kolakowski was expelled from the Party, Djilas and Mihailov were put in prison and effectively silenced. Dubcek has been dethroned and his adherents scattered and reduced to utter impotence. All the same, their ideas have already entered the public domain. It is not impossible that someone who has absorbed them and carried doubts in the recesses of his mind for many years might one day find himself in a leading position, so that while he appeared to be a Communist on the way up he would turn out not to be one once he had arrived. How could one know that this was the case?

Changes in personal convictions of this type would be immaterial if they did not manifest themselves in actions. A group of no-longer-Communists could change the nature of the regime most expediently by ceasing and desisting from policies which they could abandon without endangering their own political security. The Kremlin, for instance, could give up antireligious propaganda, the regimentation of art and literature, anti-American campaigns, without jeopardizing the country's political stability. Similarly, it could reduce and eventually abolish compulsory Communist indoctrination in the educational system. All this could be accomplished without any political detriment. Another series of steps might be still more daring; for instance, the administration of the economy, particularly agriculture, apart from ideological preconceptions, and the granting of considerable freedom in publications. If all this were to amount to an undoing of the Communist tyranny, it would eventually have to culminate in political freedom, the respect for values and principles spontaneously embraced by people articulated in society. One can never be sure that Communism has come to an end until it has either relinquished or effectively lost its monopoly of power and organization. To the extent to which we confront Communists with this criterion as our ultimate demand, we should in all fairness recognize that it constitutes a course of great danger to those who would embark on it, and beyond that to an entire country, which might easily plunge into chaos. Thus one might do well to be content with less, as an earnest of real change. There is one step that would both signal to the world the end of the Communist ideology and avoid leading Russia to the brink of political dissolution: that step is the abandonment of the Communist teaching that history has "inexorable laws" and that the socialist future is virtually a present certainty. Socialism conceived in idealistic terms of a desired moral quality of social relations does not require a dogma of historical inevitability. It is the Communist thesis of the class struggle as the road to that future which commits the Party to an irreconcilable hostility against the West, because the Party must assume that only the West stands in the way of history's beneficial climax. The giving up of this thesis would not compel people in Sovietland to drop their preference for socialism in so far as they have it; to demand this would probably build up immovable psychological barriers to change. A former Communist having happily come to power in Moscow could make it abundantly clear that he no longer is committed to such mythical notions as historical inevitability and protracted struggle but regards socialism simply as his country's preference and would accept other countries with their preferences without any hostility. Such a declaration would be tantamount to a declaration of peace and would indeed pave the way for a significant "lessening of international tensions."

The Need for Cold War Goals

It is extremely important to realize that we can help to prepare the way for such changes by making clear what we expect and do not expect. So far, we have done nothing of the sort. On the contrary, we have acted on the manifest assumption that we are willing to accept Communism with its present hostility to us and its global aggressiveness and that, without requiring any change, we are willing to make unilateral concessions in order to buy a little temporary truce. With regard to the desired end of Communism we have been sentimental and subjective, projecting our wish into realities that are quite contrary. Inasmuch as we have frequently stated our conviction that Communism is here to stay we have actively discouraged change. Communism, however, is not here to stay, for it is an enterprise of a very small number of people, at the most no more than forty million in the entire world, and those spread over many countries. It will one day crumble and become ineffective, and that day is mankind's best hope to escape atomic devastation as well as destructive tyranny. The problem of change in Communism therefore must be thought through with the utmost effort. Let us distinguish trivial and superficial changes from fundamental mutations. Let us speculate seriously and intelligently about the various ways in which the latter might produce themselves. And let us assist potential mutation through clear ideas about the things which contribute to the peace of the world.